W9-BCC-534

Linguistics
and the
Teaching
of
English

INDIANA UNIVERSITY STUDIES

IN THE

HISTORY AND THEORY OF LINGUISTICS

EDITORIAL COMMITTEE

THOMAS A. SEBEOK, Indiana University, CHAIRMAN

CHARLES A. FERGUSON, Center for Applied Linguistics

ERIC P. HAMP, University of Chicago

DELL H. HYMES, University of Pennsylvania

JOHN LOTZ, Columbia University

LINGUISTICS AND THE TEACHING OF ENGLISH

Albert Henry Marckwardt

Indiana University Press

Bloomington

London

All rights reserved
Copyright © 1966 by Indiana University Press
Library of Congress catalog card number: 67-10105
Manufactured in the United States of America

Contents

One. The English Teacher and the Science of Language   3

Two. Current Approaches to English Grammar   7

Three. Usage: Varieties, Levels, and Styles   27

Four. Usage: Finding and Interpreting the Facts   48

Five. Linguistics and the Teaching of Composition   66

Six. Linguistics and the Teaching of Spelling and Reading   85

Seven. Linguistics and the Study of Literature   100

Eight. The Role of Language in the Curriculum   122

Notes   139

Index   147

420,7
M333 l

97461

Linguistics
and the
Teaching
of
English

One

THE ENGLISH TEACHER
AND THE SCIENCE
OF LANGUAGE

OVER THE PAST TWO DECADES EDUCATION IN THIS COUNTRY, and indeed elsewhere, has felt the impact of two explosions: an explosion of population and an explosion of knowledge. The first has resulted in an increase in the number of children to be taught, often without a corresponding expansion of facilities. The second has made it necessary to teach more subjects and more about the familiar subjects, also without a corresponding increase in the time necessary to perform this extended task.

In each of the various disciplines—mathematics, science, social studies, foreign languages—knowledge has expanded rapidly. In addition, new approaches and new methods of teaching these subjects have been developed. In mathematics, not only parents but teachers are bedeviled by the unfamiliarity of what is in many of the current textbooks. In physics, the basic concepts and their attendant vocabulary bear little resemblance to what was current even as recently as two decades ago. The social sciences are turning more and more to conclusions based upon quantitative data, and in other areas cultural relativity calls for a revision of hitherto unquestioned assumptions and points of view. Foreign-language study has been revamped in the direction of greater emphasis upon mastery of the spoken language and now occupies a somewhat more prominent place in the curriculum than it has had for some years. In the case of English, the teachers of this subject, like their colleagues in other departments, are faced with a multitude of recent developments in the systematic study of language. They too must come to grips with an increase in the totality of knowledge, new concepts, and new approaches. They can take some cold comfort from the realization that they are by no means alone.

In each of these instances there arises the question of how much of what is new should be put into the subject as it is presented in the secondary schools. And quite as important, how much of what is new should the teacher be aware of, even though he may not teach it directly. The answers to such questions are by no means simple, nor are they necessarily the same for every school subject. In many of the sciences, recent developments have rendered incorrect some of the information, and beyond that even the basic assumptions, which used to be presented. A table of chemical elements and their atomic weights drawn from a chemistry textbook of the 1920's would now be obsolete. In physics the general survey of all branches of the science is often replaced by an approach in depth in one or two fields. The social studies, too, are faced with the difficult issue of breadth versus depth: how to deal with the multitude of factors operating upon man in society; how to present at least some of the salient characteristics of cultures other than our own without permitting the entire subject to degenerate into a series of puerile syntheses and unsupported generalizations.

Teachers of the foreign languages, including Latin, have somewhat more in common with those of us whose responsibility it is to develop skill in the use of the native language, perceptiveness in understanding it, and sensitivity to its qualities. Both deal with a body of content for which a natural language is the vehicle of communication. In each instance the development of skill in the employment of the language is a fundamental aim. In both the native and the foreign language field, programs for the preparation of teachers have given no more than a minimum of time and attention to the assumptions, the ideas, and the attitudes concerning language which have been developing and the mass of information which has come to light during the present century, in short that body of knowledge and systematic procedure of study which we have come to know as linguistics. It must be admitted, however, that we have moved farther and faster in applying the current ideas and new developments to the teaching of most foreign languages than to the teaching of English as a native language. We have, incidentally, done rather well with English as a foreign language, but that is a quite different story.

There are many reasons for this lag in the application of linguistics to the teaching of English, most of them having to do with the greater complexity of the teaching situation, a factor which scarcely needs elaboration. English as a school subject has many facets. Language is involved in one way or another in every one of them. As a result, there is not just one or one kind of application of linguistics, the systematic study of language, to the varied activities of the English classroom. There are, instead, potential applications to each of the components of the subject: reading, spelling, composition, literature, and so on.

These applications, or at least a presentation and discussion of some which I believe to be feasible, will constitute the material of the chapters which are to follow. I shall avoid technicalities and abstract theory as much as I can. My intention is merely to furnish the serious and professionally dedicated teacher with some food for thought. I shall not attempt to sell linguistics by suggesting that it will furnish quick and easy answers to problems which have been plaguing English teachers for years. To do so would be patently dishonest.

Nevertheless, there can be no question about the value for every teacher of becoming acquainted with various ways of looking at language which have engaged the attention of steadily increasing numbers of scholars and students over the past three decades and especially the last ten years. I have been most careful here not to say *one* way or *a* way of looking at language. But let us not lose sight of the point which was made at the beginning of this introductory chapter. The necessity of having to catch up with the advances in a particular section or division of the subject-matter field is by no means confined to the English-teaching profession. It is a common complaint and a common challenge to educators everywhere.

Two

CURRENT APPROACHES
TO ENGLISH GRAMMAR

MANY STRANGE CONCEPTIONS AND MISCONCEPTIONS HAVE BE-
come centered about grammar, both as a word and as a way of
studying language. For one thing, the general public believes
that all teachers of English have mastered this subject, one which
it conceives to be somewhat esoteric. It assumes, moreover, that
by virtue of such a mastery, every English teacher is thereby
enabled to speak and write in a manner that is not only correct
but even elegant. Indeed, the very knowledge that one is a teacher
of English will, upon occasion, embarrass those with whom he
engages in conversation. They will apologize for their own inepti-
tude in their native tongue and accordingly feel, or claim to feel,
certain constraints upon their natural instincts toward self-
expression. "So you're an English teacher. I'll have to watch my
grammar." So much for the folklore. Now what about the fact?

We must recognize, first of all, that throughout much of the
educational history of the Western world, the role of grammar
in the curriculum has been both shrinking and changing its focus.
In the medieval universities the trivium, or curriculum for the
baccalaureate, consisted of just three subjects: grammar, logic,
and rhetoric. Thus it would be fair to say that the entire program

for the A.B. seven centuries ago was the science and art of communication, now relegated to a single course or at most two in the college freshman year. At a lower educational level, there were grammar schools in the Middle Ages and the Renaissance, so called because there too grammar was predominant in the curriculum. But it was there primarily as a tool for the study of Latin, and later on for Greek as well.

Notice the differences which three or four hundred years have brought about. In the schools of today, at least in the United States, grammar is presumed to be a tool for the study of English first of all, and for other languages secondarily. Here, then, is the shift of focus. Because many have expressed doubts about its effectiveness in the improvement of native language skills, little room has been left in the English curriculum for the study of grammar *per se*. The time given to it has been drastically reduced in favor of what is frequently referred to as functional grammar.

This latter term is often employed but seldom defined. An explanation of it would undoubtedly be something like the following: There are possibly somewhere between 60 and 200 items of usage which the schools feel it their obligation to correct or eliminate. These would range all the way from such clearly non-prestigious forms as *ain't* and *lay* for *lie* to the use of *real* as an intensive or *like* as a subordinating conjunction, the latter two often being normal responses in the language of teacher and student alike—I shall deal at a later time with the current status of some of these. At any rate, in attempting to cope with such errors, real or supposed, the teacher employing a so-called functional approach rationalizes each of them on the basis of a particular rule or axiom: *real* is an adjective, not an adverb, and thus may not be used to modify adjectival or adverbial forms; therefore *real good* is incorrect. Although each offending form is explained away in a fashion analogous to this, it is not considered worthwhile taking the time to give the student a full and coherent view of the way in which his language is put together and the way it functions.

Just as the efficacy of formal grammar has been questioned, so too has the effectiveness of functional grammar. It is very difficult to prove a case either way. Both its attackers and its defenders have depended upon dubious statistics derived from imperfectly controlled experimental situations, in which highly questionable instruments of evaluation were employed. On other occasions, positions pro and con have been justified in terms of doubtful analogies. Our purpose here, however, is not to express a judgment about functional grammar but rather to explain what it is and how it came to supersede the earlier, more formal, approach.

Over the past few years, however, a number of circumstances have combined to raise two questions. First, should the systematic study of the English language occupy a somewhat larger share of the curriculum than it has over the past two or three decades? Second, if the answer to the preceding question is yes, or even a qualified yes, what kind of grammar is to be taught?

At this point we encounter a strange and not wholly consistent attitude among English teachers. In general they are quite prepared to accept the obvious fact that literary critics disagree with one another, sometimes violently, over the merits of a particular literary work, or even the bases upon which it should be judged. English teachers are equally aware of disagreements among historians, philosophers, and poets, for that matter. Yet they are most reluctant to grant the same privilege to linguistic scholars. From them the English teacher seems to have no hesitation in demanding a set of unanimously agreed upon answers to a host of pressing and practical questions. Here are some of them: Is the teacher to abandon whatever grammar he has been teaching, presumably employing a conventional or traditional approach?

If so, with what shall he replace it? If new material of some kind is the answer, how will it differ from the old? Must he learn a new terminology? Must there be several new approaches to grammar? Why not just one that everyone will agree upon? Will a new kind of grammar be more effective in improving the language of his students?

These questions have become so pressing that at least one issue per year of the *English Journal* and of *College English* are devoted almost entirely to them. Workshops and discussion sessions on linguistic problems at the annual meetings of the National Council of Teachers of English and the Conference on College Composition and Communication have multiplied more rapidly than those devoted to any other subject related to English teaching. Even on the state level, the NCTE affiliates are paying considerable attention to language matters.

We must not, however, delude ourselves into thinking that such problems are either wholly current or wholly American. The following quotation will demonstrate that even a century ago teachers had been finding grammar pretty dull fare.

> From the plan thus briefly explained, it will be perceived that the main design of this work is to exhibit a method of instruction which may relieve the monotony and *mechanical drudgery* usually attending the study of grammar, not by *innovations* and *novelties* but by a simple and natural course of exercises, which, if properly attended to, will not only ensure thorough knowledge in the progress of the subject, but will teach the method by which the language may be studied with the greatest pleasure and advantage, and by which it can be employed with the most strength and propriety.[1]

It is less than likely, of course, that Weld's method preserved all the virtues that he claimed for it, otherwise we would be employing it today.

Another statement which will surely be of interest to American teachers is to be found in the eighth report of the Secondary School Examinations Council of the Department of Education and Science in Great Britain, published in 1964. In justifying a change in university entrance requirements, the authors of the report explain:

> The decisions of the universities of Oxford and Cambridge to introduce a sixth form test in English language into their entrance requirements was based upon the conclusion of their Committees that "far too high a proportion of undergraduates at the time of their matriculation find undue difficulty in expressing themselves accurately and clearly in their own language."[2]

To these words of the joint committee, the group representing Oxford University added, "The standard of English appears to us to be in general regrettably low in the country as a whole." This statement will have a familiar ring to the English teachers in this country, weary from their efforts to cope with the problems of language instruction in overcrowded classes, and burdened with unrealistic teaching schedules. They are accustomed to hearing the death knell of the English language tolled with monotonous regularity. What is particularly surprising about this statement is that it comes from England.

Thus it is that teachers have become concerned over the problems of language instruction and the place of grammar in it. And this is why, as I have previously indicated, the professional journals and organizations are devoting more and more attention, year by year, to discussions of linguistics and grammar.

Currently, most discussions of grammar directed toward English teachers recognize three approaches, which are labeled the traditional, the structural, and the transformational, respectively. This classification is unsatisfactory from a number of points of view. It appears to be based somewhat roughly and arbitrarily upon chronology. According to it, whatever in the way of analysis or description of English was produced prior to 1933, the date of Bloomfield's *Language,* is called traditional. The period between 1933 and 1957, the date of Chomsky's *Syntactic Structures,* is thought of as being dominated by the structural grammarians, and for the work of Chomsky, his associates and his disciples, the terms transformational and generative are quite indiscriminately employed. The general tendency is to look upon each of these as distinct from the others, much as one might regard the advice of three physicians prescribing different remedies for the ailing patient. In the light of such a concept, it is small wonder that many teachers are inclined to consider seriously the possibility of ignoring them all and letting nature take its course. Needless to say, there is something wrong both with such a conclusion and with the classification which gives rise to it. Certainly each of the three categories merits a careful examination.

To a degree at least the term *traditional* seems to be used in a dual sense. Narrowly considered, it refers to the general approach to grammar which has been employed in the schools of this country from the time of Lindley Murray to the present. His *Grammar of the English Language Adapted to the Different Classes of Learners,* first published in 1795, went through hundreds of editions and sold millions of copies in its time. Despite changes in format—better print and more attractive covers—Murray's mode of analysis and basic approach to language is still to be found in a number of school texts and college freshman handbooks on the market today. Drill sentences have been updated, illustrative material is drawn from the contemporary scene, but all of this amounts to little more than pouring old wine into new bottles.

Aside from reflecting what has been for a long time the prevalent pattern in American textbooks and classroom procedure, this kind of grammar is traditional in that it represents the continuation of a way of studying language which had its beginnings with Plato and was continued in the works of Aristotle, Posidonius, Dionysius Thrax, Varro, and Priscian. Although as we shall see, traditional grammar admits of more variation than many are likely to suspect, still the basic classification and terminology had developed into something like their present form by the sixth century.

Since the term is used very loosely at times, it will be worth our while to examine some of the characteristics of this so-called traditional approach. In the first place the word *grammar* itself comes from the Greek *gramma,* meaning "letter." This suggests what was in fact true, that traditional grammar was based upon the written language. Lily, the celebrated Renaissance grammarian, whose work bore the imprimatur of King Henry VIII of England, defined grammar as the art of writing and speaking correctly. He was careful to place writing first; this is significant rather than accidental. Goold Brown in his compendious *Grammar of English Grammars* explained the reason for this initial and almost total concern with writing:

> For it ought to be remembered that over any fugitive colloquial dialect which has never been fixed by visible signs, grammar has no control; and that the speaking which the art or science of grammar teaches, is exclusively that which has reference to a knowledge of letters.[3]

Even as late as 1943, a volume prepared for the U.S. Armed Forces Institute, intended, so it said, to teach its soldier-students not schoolmarm's English but "clear, straight, he-man English," was careful to say, "Mainly this book will help your writing, though it should also help your speech." Thus the tradition of primary concern with the written language continues down to the present day.

A second feature of traditional grammar, particularly from the point of view of its use in the schools, is its emphasis upon syntax. In English, of course, there are not many inflections to deal with, and although phonology is given some consideration, it is rarely thought of as having anything to do with the structure. As early as 1703, Robert Johnson in his *Grammatical Commentaries* spoke of the relation of words to each other in sentences as constituting the most essential part of grammar. It is quite possible that much of the strength which still adheres to the traditional approach lies precisely here. Many of the practical problems in student writing do concern the ordering of words in sentences and their relation to each other. The very fact that traditional grammar deals with these matters in a familiar terminology, employing concepts with which the teacher is familiar, makes him reluctant to try anything different despite some of its obvious shortcomings.

With any grammar or kind of grammar there is always the question of how one employs it as a corrective device, how to proceed from the grammar to the improvement of the language. Here traditional grammar does not differ markedly in basic assumption from other kinds of language analysis, although in procedure it is perhaps a bit more negative. The basic premise is that a thorough knowledge of the structure of English will enable the student to identify error and thus to improve his command of the language. Originally, parsing was the mechanism designed to achieve this end; it adhered to a fairly rigid formula. For example, given the incorrect sentence, "The man is prudent which speaks little," the student was supposed to respond:

This sentence is incorrect because *which* is a pronoun of the neuter gender and does not agree in gender with its antecedent *man,* which is masculine. But a pronoun should agree with its antecedent in gender, according to the fifth rule of syntax. *Which* should therefore be *who,* a relative pronoun agreeing with its antecedent *man* and the sentence should stand thus, "The man is prudent who speaks little."[4]

The strong commitment to deduction, implemented as we have seen by parsing, is evident here. Early in the nineteenth century there had been some experimentation with an inductive procedure in teaching grammar, but it apparently made little headway. Goold Brown gave the idea short shrift. He wrote: "But in teaching grammar, to desert the plain method of definition and example, rule and praxis, and to pretend to lead children by philosophic induction into a knowledge of words is to throw down the ladder of learning that boys may imagine themselves to ascend it, while they are merely stilting over the low level upon which its fragments are cast." The tone of this and what follows is not unlike some of the fulminations against progressive education, which were to come a century later.

Though we may call it traditional, we must not delude ourselves into thinking that there was anything like complete agreement with respect to this kind of grammar. For example, certain eighteenth-century grammarians, such as James Harris and James Buchanan, assumed the existence of a universal grammar, founded in universal reason, with its purest embodiment in the language of Greek and Latin authors. This was by no means generally accepted. Again Goold Brown's comment represents a typical caveat: "Universal or Philosophical Grammar is a large field for speculation and inquiry and embraces many things which though true in themselves are unfit to be incorporated with any system of practical grammar however comprehensive its place."[5]

Nor is there, among the traditional grammarians, anything like a consensus as to the number and the names of the parts of speech to be applied to the English language. Even in the nineteenth century the number ranged all the way from three to ten. One threefold system recognized nouns, verbs, and particles; another substituted the adjective for the particle. One four-part scheme consisted of nouns, verbs, articles, and conjunctions; a second of nouns, adnouns, verbs, and particles. The most elaborate division, that into ten parts, was as follows: article, noun, adjective, pronoun, verb, participle, adverb, conjunction, preposition, and interjection. The mere fact of disagreement, of course, does not in itself constitute an objection to this or any other approach; in fact it may be evidence of health and vigor in a discipline. The principal reason for bringing up the matter is that those who today are inclined to favor traditional grammar often do so in part because they believe it to be a stable body of doctrine.

What are the objections which have been raised against this kind of traditional grammar? There have been three in particular. First, the grammarians of this school maintained a somewhat hidebound position on usage. They tended to accept as correct whatever was in conformity with the rules, abstractly and logically derived, and to reject any usage which failed to fit the rule, irrespective of the position, social prestige, or literary reputation of the person who employed it. This rejection of usage, a phenomenon of eighteenth-century England, has been dealt with in detail by S. A. Leonard, Charles C. Fries, and others; it need not be repeated here.

The very structure of English created another problem. As we have seen, traditional grammar was derived in the main from analyses and descriptions of Greek and Latin, both highly inflected languages. Since this was the case, it was possible to identify the various parts of speech, to recognize case, tense, mood, person, and number forms by means of formal characteristics, namely the inflectional suffixes: *-ibus* and *-ōrum* identified Latin ablative and genitive plurals respectively; *-ant* and *-ātur* were found only in verbs, and so on. Because English had so very few inflections, it became necessary to define the parts of speech in other terms. At times meaning was used, as in the traditional definitions of noun and verb, and on other occasions function served as the basis—the adjective modifies; the conjunction connects. This inevitably led to confusion. Such terms as pronominal adjective and conjunctive adverb are in themselves striking evidence of a multiple system of classification.

The concepts and definitions based upon meaning were especially liable to involvement in a kind of logical circularity which is aptly illustrated by the following parsing model of the sentence, "Vice degrades."

> *Vice* is a common noun of the third person, singular number, neuter gender, and nominative case, and is the subject of *degrades;* according to the rule which says, "A noun or pronoun which is the subject of the verb must be in the nominative case," because the meaning is "vice degrades."[6]

An excellent summation of the case against traditional grammar is to be found in the report of the English Secondary School Examinations Council, which was referred to earlier in this chapter. It reads as follows:

> Traditional methods of studying the English language in secondary schools have not been wholly effective. The treatment of the structure of the language has often been based upon grammatical rules derived from classical Latin or from abstract theories based upon insufficient knowledge of language development, which are inappropriate to modern English. Examinations at ordinary level have naturally followed the same pattern and so have tended to prolong a misdirected method of teaching

which assumes that a living language is subject to a single set of rules of correctness and incorrectness, regardless of style or occasion.[7]

It is important to differentiate clearly between the kind of traditional grammar which has just been described and the historically and philologically oriented approach to the subject, characteristic of a number of grammatical works which appeared for the most part during the first quarter of the present century. At times these are also classified as traditional; actually they are quite the opposite. Henry Sweet and Otto Jespersen may be taken as representative of the philological-historical school, but there were others as well. Their work differs from that of the traditional grammarians in a number of significant ways.

To begin with, they began to pay a considerable amount of attention to phonology, that is, to the entire sound system of the language. This was what might normally have been expected of Sweet, the original of Professor Henry Higgins in George Bernard Shaw's *Pygmalion.* And indeed in the Preface of this *New English Grammar,* published in 1891, we find the comment, "An essential feature of this grammar is that it is on a phonetic basis. It is now generally recognized, except in hopelessly obscurantist circles, that phonology is the indispensable foundation of all linguistic study, whether practical or scientific."[8] The entire first volume of Otto Jespersen's eight-volume *A Modern English Grammar* (with the significant subtitle *On Historical Principles*) was devoted to English pronunciation, present and past. In works such as these, contracted forms were recognized as normal occurrences in the language rather than stigmatized as unfortunate inelegancies. The shift of stress in otherwise similar pairs as *ob'ject* (noun) and *ob·ject'* (verb) was seen as part of the functioning mechanism of the language. This tendency may be said to have had its culmination with the appearance in 1928 of Harold E. Palmer's *A Grammar of Spoken English*.[9]

At least some of the grammarians representing this general approach felt that the traditional part-of-speech classification was of limited usefulness in describing the structure of English. Jespersen was one of them. "It will be seen that the distinction between different parts of speech always depends on formal criteria," he commented, and then went on to say, "On the other hand, it must be recognized that such formal criteria are not always present with the same degree of clearness, and Modern English in many cases has obliterated distinctions that were formerly more evident."[10] Although he did use the old terms and concepts to some extent, he depended to a much greater degree upon a hierarchical system based upon the degree of specificity of meaning and application. Thus in the combination *extremely hot weather, weather* was called a primary word or principal, *hot* a secondary word or adjunct, and *extremely* a tertiary word or subjunct. He also distinguished between junction and nexus as two distinct ways of combining words, the first of which representing what we might think of as adjective-noun combinations and the second the noun-verb relationship. There were also other experiments with grammatical classification and description. Janet R. Aiken in *A New Plan of English Grammar*[11] proposed a classification based upon six grammatical functions instead of eight parts of speech.

Finally, these historically and philologically oriented grammarians were much less inclined than their predecessors to reject as incorrect, illiterate, or slovenly the usages which did not fit the rules they had formulated. They made a careful examination at least of literary usage, and employed an essentially inductive procedure. "It must be borne in mind," wrote Henry Sweet in

1891, "that rules of grammar have no value except as statements of facts: whatever is in general use in a language is for that very reason grammatically correct."[12] The scholarly grammars that were written from this point of view, such as those of Jespersen and, in this country, of George O. Curme, contain a wealth of illustrative material which is still useful. It is interesting to observe that a good many of them were written by foreigners: Jespersen was a Dane; Kruisinga and Poutsma were from Holland. Many of the important works were known only or chiefly by scholars and had little impact on textbooks in this country. Both the authors and the work they produced differed totally in content and spirit from the truly traditional grammarians; they should not be classed together merely upon the basis of date. Actually, such men as Sweet and Jespersen, because of the spirit in which they operated, did much to pave the way for the next group in point of time, namely the structuralists.

The structuralists represent an intellectual tradition and an approach which may be said to have its sources in the work of de Saussure, the Prague School of linguistics, Edward Sapir, and Leonard Bloomfield, although these scholars were by no means always in complete agreement with each other. Nevertheless, those who became aligned with this movement felt that it represented something as wholly new and different as the Copernican astronomy replacing the Ptolemaic. It seems somewhat less so now, perhaps, as we look at it in historical perspective, but to many an English teacher reared on the concepts of traditional grammar it still smacks of heresy and revolution.

To attempt to deal with structuralism with anything like adequate detail would almost necessitate the writing of a history of linguistic science over the past twenty-five years. This is manifestly impossible here. What is most important for the teacher today is to be able to attach some meaning to the word *structural* and to identify the principal characteristics of this approach which distinguish it from what went before. This may be done most effectively by beginning with the definition of language employed by many of the structuralists. A typical form of it runs somewhat as follows: Language is socially conditioned, patterned vocal behavior by means of which humans are enabled to cooperate in society. The definition may vary slightly at times, but the ideas remain much the same. Virtually every word in it has its particular function and contributes to the structuralist view of language.

For the purpose here, two features of the definition are especially important. First of all, language is viewed as vocal behavior, which implies that writing is a secondary or derived form of it. Unfortunately the structuralists did not always succeed in explaining just what they meant by this, and a considerable amount of misunderstanding has resulted.

In addition, the definition characterizes the vocal behavior as being patterned. The task of the grammarian, therefore, becomes one of describing the patterns of which the language consists, as they are manifested primarily in speech and secondarily in writing. Thus the concept of pattern or structure came to be sought in all aspects of language. For example, in one analysis of English phonology, the simple vowel phonemes were described in terms of an articulatory matrix that recognizes three degrees of jaw height and three degrees of tongue position. Moreover, each of the nine simple vowels was able to combine with any one of three semivowels to form a vowel-semivowel nucleus. This is pattern. The morphophonemic alternation of the noun plural inflection, with [s] after voiceless consonants (*cats*), [z] after voiced sounds (*dogs, pianos*), and [əz] after sibilants (*noses, churches*) is another instance of patterned behavior. So, too, is the fact that an affirmative question tag follows a negative statment (He isn't coming, *is he?*) whereas an affirmative statement is followed by a negative tag (He's coming, *isn't he?*). In short, the structuralists see pattern in the sounds of language, the inflections, and the syntax.

Pervading all of this was the attempt to maintain procedural rigor by working inductively from the form or external manifestation to the meaning or internal significance. By holding in abeyance certain parts of the familiar, traditional grammatical analysis, heavily Latin and Greek based as we have seen, the structuralists succeeded in directing attention to many features and distinctions of the system which had hitherto been ignored. For example, question words such as *where* or *when,* uttered in response to an affirmative statement ("I'm going downtown." "Where?") were recognized as calling for repetition when they had a rising intonation but for more specific information when spoken with a falling intonation. Valid generalizations were worked out for the order of several modifiers preceding a noun: *all the ten fine old gray stone houses.* From this point of view, the structuralists discovered much about the behavior of the language which was fresh and new—but much of it was felt by the classroom teacher of English to be somewhat remote from his practical concerns.

But even in the analysis of English during this period, the structuralists by no means represented a united front. Professor Raven I. McDavid, Jr., has described them as consisting of two major camps, the descriptive analytic and the descriptive synthetic. "The first," he says, "seeks to show what are the constituents of larger structures; the second, how larger structures may be made out of smaller ones."[13] As an instance of the first group, *The Structure of English* by Charles C. Fries comes immediately to mind. He begins with the total utterance, seeking to analyze it in terms of the recurrent parts or particles which go to make it up. The opposite approach is to be found in such works as *An Outline of English Structure* by George L. Trager and Henry Lee Smith, Jr., and *Introduction to Linguistic Structures* by A. A. Hill. They begin their analyses with the smallest units of speech, the phonemes, proceed next to the morpheme or minimum unit of form, arriving at the complete utterance only as a final step.

From the point of view of the classroom teacher, the principal shortcomings of the structuralists were to be found in the uncertain way in which syntax was handled, especially in the relationship of the component or constituent parts to each other. On a lower level of complexity, it was easy enough to see that *unladylike* consisted of the prefix *un-* combined with *ladylike,* rather than *unlady* plus *-like,* and to recognize that *old men and women* may be divided in two different ways. But as one moved into the consideration of more complicated utterances, there seemed to be no consistent basis for making the divisions and indicating their relationship to each other.

It was in large part this particular weakness of the structuralist approach which led to the development of generative grammar. For many teachers in this country, the name chiefly associated with it is that of Noam Chomsky, whose monograph *Syntactic Structures*[14] has been widely read and commented on. Nevertheless, the work of Robert B. Lees, Paul M. Postal, and Morris Halle must also be described or classified as generative. Moreover, there are other recent departures from the strictly structuralist approach, represented by the stratificational grammar of Sidney Lamb and the neo-Firthian position of Michael Halliday. What is of greater importance than distinguishing among these various schools is to resolve the confusion between the terms *generative* and *transformational* when used in connection with them.

The term *generative* applies to the aim of grammatical study or of an individual grammar, which is here presumed to be productive rather than analytical. In short, the grammar of a language will, to quote Chomsky, "be a device that generates all of the grammatical sequences of a language and none of the ungrammatical ones." This is achieved by a series of explicit procedures or so-called "rules" presented as formulas. Thus T + N + V + NP is a rule which will "produce" a phrase structure such as *The man hit the ball* or *The boy studied the lesson.*

But, the generative grammarians point out, a grammar confined to the description or formulization of phase structures is often incapable of discriminating between such sentences as *He was parked by a stream* and *He was elected by a landslide.* On this point Chomsky comments:

> We can greatly simplify the description of English and gain new and important insight into its formal structure if we limit the direct description in terms of phrase structure to a kernel of basic sentences (simple, declarative, active, with no complex verb or noun phrases), deriving all other sentences from these . . . by transformation, possibly repeated.[15]

Accordingly, there are formulas which convert *John eats the apple* to *The apple is eaten by John, Did John eat the apple?, John didn't eat the apple,* and *What did John eat?* Transformation is thus a device or operation, but, as we have seen, the term *generative* refers to aim.

Transformations are useful in differentiating such structural similarities as *the growling of lions* and *the raising of flowers.* These are alike in phrase structure but nevertheless represent totally different kinds of relationships with respect to their principal elements. *The growling of lions* may be viewed as a metamorphosed form of *Lions growl* whereas a similar transposition of *the raising of flowers* would be meaningless; it must be seen as a transformation of *They raise flowers.* Viewed in this manner, the structural ambiguity of *the shooting of the hunters* is immediately apparent. It could be a transformation of either of the preceding patterns.

Generative grammar constitutes the most recent development in the field of language description and a highly interesting one. Since it does come to grips with syntax directly, it has had a somewhat more favorable reception among teachers than some varieties of structural grammar, although some of the comments in the pedagogical journals and educational research monographs do betray a certain lack of understanding. One misconception in particular is so widespread that it must be dealt with here, namely the notion that a transformation formula describes a psychological process. It will be helpful to see what a generative grammarian has to say on this point:

> Transformations are often erroneously conceived to be direct descriptions of processes that a speaker follows in constructing sentences (the same statement holds for generative theories as a whole). The investigation of how speakers actually construct or understand sentences is properly the concern of psychology or psycholinguistics. . . . A transformation is basically a statement of certain relations holding between structures in a grammar. It is introduced because such a rule can do things which simpler rules cannot do (or can do only in a clumsy manner).[16]

From what has gone before in this chapter, it is evident that there is no one single and infallible approach to an understanding of the structure of English. There is no one grammar; there are many. No single grammar is a clear and complete answer to the question of how the English language is put together and how it operates, nor is it an unequivocal answer to the question, "What shall I teach?"

Before the teacher can begin to answer this last question, there is the even more fundamental one, "What and how much should I know?" The answer to this is, "A great deal, in fact as much as possible of each of these grammars." He must know enough to evaluate the textbook he uses and the curriculum in which he teaches. He must master these rather than run the risk of being mastered and dictated to by them. A textbook and the grammar which it contains must be a tool which he is able to use as his intelligence dictates, to adapt to the immediate purpose, to add to or subtract from. He can do this only by familiarizing himself with what has been thought and said about the English language. It is not an easy task, but gaining knowledge and imparting skill is never easy. It always demands even more of the teacher than of the student.

Three

USAGE:

VARIETIES, LEVELS,

AND STYLES

WE MAY AS WELL FACE IT! AMERICANS ARE ESSENTIALLY PRAG-matists, and this applies to education as well as to many other facets of our national life. Almost our first question concerning any school subject is, "What is it good for?" or "How can it be used?" I believe that I am safe in saying that the one subject that simply could not be eliminated from the school curriculum today, no matter how strong the conviction or indignation of the re-former, would be driver education. Nor do I for one particularly want to remove it.

I make this point for two reasons. First, no matter how much we may argue in theory that language is a legitimate part of the subject matter or content of English, and that therefore a sys-tematic presentation of the structure of the English language merits inclusion at various places in the elementary and sec-ondary curriculum, the interest of most teachers is likely to be focused upon the improvement of the language of their students with respect to specific items or features of usage. The fact that a systematic study of grammar appeared not to be effective in

attaining these ends was responsible for its progressive diminu-
tion in the curriculum throughout the first half of the present
century.

Moreover, I think it is by no means an accident that what may
be characterized as the battle of usage, namely the struggle for
a more realistic and more reasonable presentation of specific
items of English usage, which the schools felt themselves committed to teach, was fought and at least partly won before the
battle of grammar, namely the carving out of a place for the
systematic study of the structure of the language, was even begun.
This is partly historical accident, I concede, but it is also in keeping with our general educational outlook.

My comments on this score should not be interpreted as criticism of the English-teaching profession. In view of the social
and cultural situation which has prevailed ever since our nation
gained its independence, and to a degree even before that, our
concern with specific features of the prestige dialect of American
English is a perfectly natural one. For decades before and after
the date of our national independence, British travelers had
looked down their noses at American linguistic innovation and
American linguistic practices which deviated from those currently acceptable in England. What may well be the first instance
of this is to be found as early as 1735 in the account of a voyage
to Georgia by a British traveler, Francis Moore. In commenting
on the location of Savannah, he wrote, "The bank of the river
(which they in barbarous English call a bluff) is steep and about
forty-five foot perpendicular." Two hundred and thirty years
later we can note with some amusement that *bluff* has in the
meantime become standard and that Moore's employment of the
unchanged plural *foot* would today mark him as uncultivated in
most parts of this country, but this did not lessen the sting of his
comment at that time.

The anvil chorus of criticism directed against the English used in this country reached ringing proportions by the fourth and fifth decades of the last century. In 1832 Mrs. Frances Trollope, who must have viewed through a lorgnette what she called *The Domestic Manners of the Americans,* wrote that during her entire stay in this country she had seldom "heard a sentence elegantly turned and correctly pronounced from the lips of an American." There was always something either in the expression or accent, she said, that pained her feelings and shocked her taste. One year later, Captain Thomas Hamilton in his *Men and Manners in America* was equally pained and quite as violently shocked by the great amount of bad grammar in circulation and the enormous number of barbarisms, which according to him were not confined to the ignorant but come as copiously from the lips of the learned." Some three or four years before that Captain Basil Hall had been so disturbed and outraged by the English he heard on his travels that he called on Noah Webster and demanded that the aging patriarch do something about it.

It is always difficult for an emergent nation, as we were then, to cut the umbilical cord attaching it to the mother country, culturally as well as politically. When the sneers at our books, our plays, our poetry were accompanied by hoots of scorn at our ordinary talk, small wonder that as a people we developed an anxiety neurosis about it and took refuge in a body of rules about usage which were so rigid, so complete a denial of the language as it really was spoken and written, that the English themselves had quite completely rejected them.

The situation was intensified from the mid-nineteenth century onward by the arrival of large numbers of immigrants from non-English-speaking countries. In general the new arrivals were subjected to tremendous pressures for conformity, and this included language as well as other facets of behavior. I suppose for almost every immigrant nationality there was a jingle similar to that ridiculing the Dutchman with his belly full of straw, incapable of saying anything but "Yaw, yaw, yaw." The upward social mobility, so continuously characteristic of this country throughout almost its entire history, creates its share of problems with respect to language, as it does with the acquisition of other middle or upper-middle class forms of socially approved behavior.

The combination of these three forces created an overwhelming demand for guidance in specific matters or items of language usage. The ridicule and embarrassment that are so often the consequence of a linguistic or other transgression of socially approved behavior created a climate which made reliance upon instinct or principle too risky to be trusted. The *arriviste* does not take it lightly when he arrives at the dessert course with nothing but a soup spoon or a salad fork to eat it with, and he doesn't want any truck with general principle; he wants to know exactly and specifically how to behave the next time he is faced with the situation. And even the anti-cultural or anti-intellectual defiance of an authoritarian standard, such as might be encountered from time to time in Mark Twain and other of our excellent humorists, was just as indicative of an underlying insecurity as the pitiful bravado of the typical nineteenth-century Fourth of July oration.

I mention these matters for two reasons: to exculpate the teachers of the last century from over-much blame for the denial of common sense, linguistically speaking—the pressures upon them were enormous—and to account for one early stage in the development of a concept of usage, a development which I intend to trace in this chapter. As late almost as the beginning of the present century, there were only two colors with which to characterize the status of specific items of language usage: black and white. A locution was either civil or barbarous, right or wrong; there was no middle ground. This was true, for example, in the works of such widely read nineteenth-century writers on language as Richard Grant White or Edward S. Gould, and even in the work of their principal antagonist, Fitz-Edward Hall.

Then there came a time when the authors of textbooks on English began to treat the range of English usage in terms of a ladder-like hierarchy of levels. What might be called the basic or minimal form of the ladder consisted of three steps: Formal or Literary English at the top; a middle stage characterized as Informal or Colloquial; a bottom rung stigmatized as Vulgar or Illiterate.

This three-stage hierarchy has been expanded at different times, and in different ways. In 1927 George Phillip Krapp, in his *Knowledge of English,* recognized five levels: Literary, Formal Colloquial, General Colloquial, Popular, and Vulgar respectively. A decade later, in Whitford and Foster's *American Standards of Writing,* we find the five levels collapsed to four, namely Formal or Literary, Colloquial, Low Colloquial or Popular, and Vulgar or Illiterate. Robert Pooley in *Teaching English Usage,* 1946, went back to a five-level system, consisting of Literary, Standard Formal, Standard Informal, Homely, and Illiterate. Even some recent books continue to adhere to the hierarchical concept with but minor variations in the scheme of presentation.

It would be interesting to speculate on some of the considerations which went into the selection of the various labels and to observe the ways in which they have been defined. Unfortunately space will permit only the overall judgment that in one sense this kind of categorization had the virtue of simplicity; likewise it also had the defects of oversimplification and misrepresentation. The vertical arrangement of levels, which was always a feature of their graphic representation, and the placing of *colloquial* some-where between literary and illiterate suggested, explicitly or im-plicitly, that the spoken language is qualitatively inferior to the written, a linguistic article of faith still firmly held by the vast majority of students, most of their English teachers, and the public at large. The suggestion was reinforced by the names of such subcategories as "Low Colloquial or Popular."

Since etymologically *vulgar* and *popular* represent very much the same concept, it is interesting to observe that the pejorative process has operated with greater rapidity in the first of these two words, and it vies with *illiterate* as the tag most often used for the least prestigious level of speech. This is understandable, since in our present culture the actual illiterate constitutes so very small a part of our population, but the type of person who is likely to employ this label will want to apply it rather liberally. Slang also occasionally gets thrown into the hierarchy, usually as a part of vulgate English, which is of course sheer nonsense.

To sophisticated observers of the language, much of this seems naive, if not downright amusing. But we have already seen that teachers of English, in their attempt to clothe their students in a linguistically decent garb, faced a whole series of complex and complicated problems—practical problems. As a conse-quence, simplification as a pedagogic device occupies a range of position on a continuum immediately adjacent to oversimpli-fication as a pedagogic nemesis. The precise boundary between the two is not at all easy to determine.

For this very reason there is unquestionably some merit in a thoughtful examination of this concept of levels of usage: When did it first appear? What was its origin? And of greater and more significant interest: What has happened to the concept recently? How has it been modified?

It has already been suggested that there was little talk about levels of usage before 1925. A number of circumstances lead one to suspect that the idea, particularly its graphic representation in terms of a vertical scale, had its origin in a diagram which occurs in Sir James Murray's prefatory material to the *Oxford English Dictionary.* As such it was in reality a misapplication of what Sir James intended there. He was not employing it to define or portray levels of speech. His diagram was intended to represent vocabulary only, to suggest degrees of adaptation or naturalization of foreign words and areas of common and overlapping use for segments of the lexicon as a whole.

We have seen, too, that despite the crudities of the scale, it was undeniably an advance over the earlier commitment to an absolute dichotomy: acceptable versus unacceptable. After all, the hierarchy did offer a means of suggesting degrees of acceptability, and it seems significant that the earliest instances of the levels concept that I have been able to find occur in the works of George Phillip Krapp, and of S. A. Leonard and H. Y. Moffett,[1] all of whom seriously questioned the validity of many of the strictures on usage common in the English textbooks of their time.

So much for the origin. Our next concern is to see how this simple but fundamentally erroneous notion has been modified, particularly during the past fifteen years. It was almost inevitable that the inconsistency of this mode of classification should come to light. We can best see how this came about by considering it in terms of the sharpening and clarification of two language concepts.

The first of these has to do with the mid-point on the scale, the term *colloquial.* There is a vast discrepancy between the technical use of the term, a neutral and taxonomic one referring to the language as spoken, and the ordinary use, a pejorative one interpreting it as a low form of language to be avoided. The fact that the word has two quite different meanings is familiar enough to the linguistically sophisticated but probably not to large numbers of teachers of English, and certainly not to thousands of students whom they send to the colleges every year.

It appears from the *Oxford English Dictionary* that Dr. Samuel Johnson introduced the term into the English language. A citation drawn from his work, "To refine our language to grammatical purity and to clear it from colloquial barbarisms," illustrates very clearly indeed how the pejorative sense of the term developed. Johnson may well have intended to convey the idea that a barbarism was much more likely to be spoken than written, for he did have a strong sense of etymology, but unquestionably some of the connotation of *barbarism* rubbed off on the word he used with it. Several, though certainly not all, of the *Oxford English Dictionary* citations are similar in this respect. Thackeray, for example, refers to "the slang and colloquialisms with which we garnish our conversation." Again we are able to see how at least a mildly pejorative sense of the term was perpetuated by association. It is not surprising, therefore, that the downgraded meaning of the word *colloquial* has retained a strong hold in contemporary usage.

The forthright treatment of *colloquial* in the second edition (1934) of *Webster's New International Dictionary* gave comfort and reinforcement to those who wanted to employ it in its neutral and technical sense, and even more important, who wanted it interpreted neutrally and technically when it was used that way. Not only did the preface indicate that colloquial English was a legitimate concern of the lexicographer and the linguistic scholar, but appended to the definition of the word itself in the body of the dictionary was the statement, "Colloquial speech may be as correct as formal speech." Certainly from that time on, the neutral and technical concept of the word came increasingly to the fore, although as I have indicated, the popular meaning is still the more common. But John S. Kenyon, then pronunciation editor of the second Webster, and Thomas A. Knott, its general editor, must be given a large share of the credit for whatever rehabilitation the word has had.

I must digress here briefly to point out that advances, both in linguistic geography and in historical linguistics, and an increasing awareness of the relationship of these two divisions of language study also came to have a definite bearing upon the idea of levels, and affected particularly the lower end or base of the hierarchy. Quite early in the nineteenth century, at least some students of regional dialects came to perceive that these differed chiefly in angle of incidence, so to speak, from social dialects. Regional dialects may be regarded as being distributed horizontally over an entire language area, whereas social dialects are distributed vertically.

Further advances and refinements in the historical study of language, coming chiefly during the latter portion of the nineteenth and the early twentieth century, focused attention upon such processes as sound change, analogy, and borrowing as the forces primarily responsible for differentiating languages from a common parent and for the development of regional dialects within a language as well. It required but a little extension of the same logic to see that the emergence of social or class dialects might be explained upon the same grounds. In some instances what has become substandard English represents the older or historical form. For example the unchanged plural after numbers (*forty foot*), is a direct descendant of the Old English genitive plural used in a partitive construction, whereas the Standard English *feet* reflects a later analogical extension. At times analogy operated in one fashion in Standard English but differently on the substandard level, as in Standard English *him-*

self and substandard *hisself*. A book which could be of the greatest interest but which still remains to be written is a historical
grammar of vulgar English.

At all events, as people began to see that forms of English
other than the standard language could be studied seriously and
accounted for historically, this disposed of the notion that the
particular class dialect spoken by the nonliterate social stratum
was necessarily corrupt or debased, irrespective of how much it
or its speakers might be lacking in prestige. And as scholars
learned more about the history of languages, they also began to
understand that the emergence of the prestige dialects of English
(that of Winchester in the ninth century, of London in the four-
teenth) was a consequence of nonlinguistic factors, usually social, political, and economic, rather than because of something
inherently superior in the dialect itself.

In resuming the thread of our principal narrative, we shall see
that it was John Kenyon also who made the first direct attack
upon the notion of a single hierarchy of language levels. He did
this in a paper read before the College English Group of North-
eastern Ohio in the fall of 1947. The paper was subsequently
published in two versions: under the title "Levels of Speech and
Colloquial English," in the January, 1948, issue of the *English
Journal,* and in the October, 1948, number of *College English,*
here entitled "Cultural Levels and Functional Varieties of
English."[2]

Briefly stated, Kenyon's thesis in these articles is that the
single hierarchical arrangement so frequently employed in language and composition textbooks was, in effect, "a false combination of two distinct and incommensurable categories." This
is the core of his argument, but for our purposes I shall quote him
a little more fully:

The word *level,* when used to indicate different styles of language is a metaphor, suggesting higher or lower position, and like the terms *higher* or *lower,* figuratively implies 'better' or 'worse,' 'more desirable' or 'less desirable' and similar comparative degrees of excellence or inferiority in language.[3]

And again:

The application of the term *level* to those different styles of language that are not properly distinguished as better or worse, desirable or undesirable, creates a false impression. I confess myself guilty of this error along with some other writers. What are frequently grouped together in one class as different levels of language are often in reality false combinations of two distinct and incommensurable categories, namely *cultural levels* and *functional varieties.*[4]

A final statement:

The two groupings, *cultural levels* and *functional varieties* are not mutually exclusive categories. They are based upon entirely separate principles of classification: *culture* and *function.*[5]

He first takes up what he considers to be a proper concept of cultural level, explaining it in these terms:

Among cultural levels may be included on the lower levels, illiterate speech, narrowly local dialect, ungrammatical speech and writing, excessive and unskilful slang, slovenly and careless vocabulary and construction, exceptional pronunciations; and on the higher level, language used generally by the cultivated, clear, grammatical writing, pronunciations used by the cultivated over wide areas. The different cultural levels may be summarized in the two general classes *substandard* and *standard.*[6]

Several features of this statement merit our attention. Note that Kenyon was careful to mention both speech and writing in connection with each of the levels. "Illiterate speech" and "ungrammatical speech and writing," are parts of the inventory of the substandard in opposition to "clear grammatical writing," and "pronunciation used by the cultivated over wide areas" as features of the standard language.

Of equal importance is his selection of a reasonably neutral term for the nonprestigious variety of the language. Admittedly *substandard* is not wholly free from pejorative coloration, since the prefix does carry with it the notion of height. Nevertheless, it was a vast improvement over such terms as *illiterate, popular,* or *vulgar,* none of which had been adequately or reasonably defined.[7]

Kenyon's characterization of the two levels does raise some questions, particularly with reference to the inclusion of dialect and slang in the substandard category. His relegation of "narrowly local dialect" to the lower level makes one wonder about the position of regional dialect, broader in its dissemination than the local—a question which remains unanswered. Even more perplexing is his mention of "excessive and unskilful slang," also as a feature of substandard. What about moderate and skillful use of slang; where does it belong? Or to complicate matters still more, let us inquire about excessive but skillful slang, and moderate but unskillful? Actually slang cuts across social levels, and it was something of a mistake on Kenyon's part to include it here. Finally, by implication at least, the statement lacks any suggestion that substandard English does have its own grammar.

Nevertheless, having disposed of the cultural levels, Kenyon was now free to suggest a totally different mode of classification. He did so in these terms:

Among *functional varieties* not depending on cultural levels may be mentioned colloquial language, itself existing in different degrees of familiarity or formality, as for example familiar conversation, private correspondence, formal conversation, familiar

public address; formal platform or pulpit speech, public reading, public worship; legal, scientific, and other expository writing; prose and poetic belles lettres.[8]

He then concludes, "The term *level,* then, does not properly
belong at all to functional varieties of speech—colloquial, familiar, formal, scientific, literary language. They are equally
'good' for their respective functions, and as classifications do not
depend upon the status of the users. The different functional
varieties may roughly be grouped together in the two classes
familiar and *formal* speech and writing."[9]

Despite the fact that the first part of the foregoing statement
appears to recognize some four or five varieties of linguistic
function, note that Kenyon eventually boils them down to two—
familiar and formal. Just where some of the specific kinds of
language activity he mentions will fit in terms of this simple
dichotomy—for example, formal conversations and familiar
public address—is not explained; as a result there is still some
confusion here between the nature of the medium (speech or
writing) on the one hand and the general atmosphere of the
discourse, familiar or formal, on the other. In short, having
eliminated one set of intersecting categories, Kenyon permits
another to remain. In addition, his treatment makes no reference
to the structural differences between speech and writing. Nowhere is the reader told that the very imperfections of the writing
system deriving from its one-dimensional, linear nature result
in a different logical organization and a somewhat different incidence of sentence patterns from those characteristic of spoken
English.

Kenyon modestly concluded that he could scarcely hope that
his humble remonstrance would reform all future writing on
levels of English. Actually there is evidence of his two articles
having had some effect. The more enlightened handbook writers

began to treat the term *colloquial* a bit more gently, and the ladder-like diagrams of the so-called levels were in some instances replaced by interlocking circles, upon occasion arranged horizontally rather than vertically.

The next significant modification of the levels concept, by Martin Joos, came a decade later. His ideas on this score were originally set forth in a monograph, *English Language and Linguistics,* written in 1958, for students and teachers of English in Yugoslavia. Three years later they appeared a second time, in slightly altered form, in his long essay bearing the somewhat cryptic title *The Five Clocks.*[10]

In both of these he recognizes five styles of English; a style here is somewhat akin to Kenyon's functional variety, but by no means identical with it. In the earlier monograph the styles were called intimate, casual, colloquial, formal, and printable. In *The Five Clocks* he changed *colloquial* to *consultative, printable* to *frozen.* Thus the second order becomes intimate, casual, consultative, formal, and frozen. The list of sentences which follows will serve to illustrate how a particular idea or statement would be expressed in each of the five styles:

Frozen: In my opinion he is not the man whom we want.
Formal: I believe he is not the man we are looking for.
Consultative: I don't believe he's the man we're looking for.
Casual: I don't think he's our man.
Intimate: 'Fraid you've picked a lemon.

In essence, these five styles constitute a hierarchy of formality. They seem to cut across the distinction between spoken and written language, but this will require further comment later. It appears that they are based in part upon the nature of the communications situation and in part upon the number of persons involved in it. They suggest very little about the degree of cultivation of the writer. Unquestionably, Joos's change in terminology from *colloquial* to *consultative* represents a gain in precision, if I understand his idea. On the other hand, the shift from *printable* to *frozen* strikes me as something less than an improvement, and I suspect that it represents some vacillation in concept.

Possibly the most effective way to deal with this series is to begin at the center. Joos describes consultative style as the speech of educated native speakers, used when gathered in groups of from two to seven persons who have no permanent or intimate acquaintance with one another, but also have no apprehension of misunderstanding or other cause for embarrassment. Just why the qualification *educated* is necessary here, I am not certain. I should think that the less educated, or even the minimally educated, would upon occasion have to consult with one another, and I am not certain that the linguistic features of the consultative style would be materially altered by the educational level of the participants.

Joos describes the consultative style as having two defining features. First, the speaker supplies background information; he assumes that he will not be wholly understood if he neglects to do so. Second, the listener participates continuously. Joos points to some of the longer telephone conversations which Charles C. Fries used as the corpus of his *Structure of English* as examples of the consultative style. The listener participation in these, however, is often limited to single word responses, such as "Yes," "Well," and the nasals of affirmation and negation. It is quite possible that in face-to-face contact this becomes somewhat more extensive.

Casual style differs from consultative in that it pays the listener the compliment of implying that he has so much experience in common with the speaker that it becomes superfluous either to supply background information or to rely upon listener participation. With respect to background information, notice how much more knowledge in common is assumed by "our man" than "the man we're looking for." As positive marks of identification, Joos mentions the presence of elliptical forms and the use of slang as features of the casual style. In fact, he insists that ellipsis is responsible for most of the differences between the grammars of the casual and the consultative styles.

Intimate speech resembles casual in that speaker and listener have many attitudes, experiences, and much knowledge in common. Intimate speech, however, excludes what Joos calls "public information." It deals only "with what is inside the speaker's skin," and thus tends to remind the person addressed rather than to inform him. The features of the intimate style are extraction, as compared with ellipsis in the casual, jargon as compared with slang.

Joos defines extraction as a minimum pattern extracted from a sentence appropriate to the casual style. Note that *'fraid* in the specimen sentence quoted above is an extraction which has done away with the subject, verb, and the initial syllable of the adjective. Or, to go on to another instance, "Cold!" uttered by a husband sitting at the breakfast table would be an extraction from "Coffee's cold," already elliptical to a degree. Moreover, this comment, uttered in a monotone, does not tell the wife anything about the temperature of the coffee. She already knows that it is cold, since she undoubtedly prepared it and knows precisely when she did it. What "Cold," does convey is a feeling inside the speaker's skin, rather than information. So does, "Fraid you've picked a lemon."

Jargon, as the term is employed here, is to be distinguished from slang in that it is code, whereas slang is presumably figure of speech. One is private language; the other is addressed to a wider public. It must be admitted that *lemon* does not illustrate the distinction between the two particularly well. Joos goes on to say that the use of extraction and jargon is not rudeness, that on the contrary it pays the addressee the highest compliment possible among mature people. The mature insist upon some guardedness in public relationships; here there is none. The intimate style tolerates nothing of the system of another style.

In moving now to the upper end of the scale, we find that formal differs from consultative primarily in that hearer participation drops out. For the most part, this is undoubtedly forced by the very nature of the situation in which communication takes place. The group may be too large; a speaker may be uncertain of the response he is to receive. Because of this, a discourse in the formal style demands advance planning; in particular, there must be a logical sequence from one idea or group of ideas to another. Cohesion and detachment are two outstanding features of the formal style.

Proceeding from the logic to the language of the formal style, Joos points out that one feature of the highest importance remains from the basal styles, namely intonation: Pronunciation is explicit; the grammar tolerates no ellipsis. This is again evident from the specimen sentences, where the formal "I believe he is not the man we are looking for" contracts neither *is not* nor *we are* and shifts the negative from the introductory to what is logically the main clause. The words are carefully chosen, Joos goes on to say; the background information is adroitly woven into the text, often in complex sentence structures.

At the extreme of the hierarchy, the frozen style is recognized as one appropriate for declamation and for publication, differing from formal speech in having many special choices and arrangements of words. To the degree that it is intended for publication, or even for declamation perhaps, no provision can be made for the normal suprasegmental features of language. Again audience participation is lacking.

This analysis by Joos merits a careful evaluation; it has both strength and weaknesses. In essence it is an elaboration of the formal-informal distinction by Kenyon, but much more carefully and thoughtfully worked out. It takes into consideration the hearer or reader, that is to say the addressee, as well as the speaker or writer, and is thus adapted to the situation-response concept of linguistic interchange. It defines or describes degrees of formality not merely in terms of labels of general content but in terms of specific features of vocabulary and linguistic form as well. It has the additional virtue of fitting the use of slang and jargon into the scale, something which both Kenyon and the traditional levels approach bungled rather badly. Furthermore, it recognizes the important fact that a discourse need not necessarily remain within a given style. An exchange which is largely consultative in style may begin with formal preliminaries, and later on it may be spiced with from one to ten per cent of casual forms. A recognition of this potentiality of style shift is particularly important for the teaching of English as a foreign language, simply because other languages behave quite differently.

Nevertheless, there are weaknesses both in the scheme and in its presentation. We are left in some doubt as to the relation between style and cultural levels. At one point, Joos speaks of "good standard mature consultative style," and we can only assume that the term *standard* is being used with reference to a prestige form of the language. Elsewhere, as I have already indicated, he characterizes *consultative* as the speech of educated native speakers. This poses the question as to whether there might be substandard consultative, substandard casual, and so on, a question which admittedly might be irrelevant to Joos's purposes, but is none the less not without its own interest.

A similar problem arises with respect to the spoken and written forms of the language. It might be maintained with some reason, although I am certain that Joos would not agree, that the frozen style is or could be considered primarily a written version of formal. Because of the requirement of audience or addressee participation, genuine written consultative may be relatively rare, but surely there must be written casual. One is inclined to wonder also about the possibility of generating these various styles or deriving one from another by a series of transformations. Would it be possible, for example, to derive casual from consultative, principally by means of a series of morphophonemic rules, or does each style have its own set of kernel sentences?

A final difficulty is pedagogical. The five styles tend to focus attention upon and make the most revealing comments about the sectors of the language which now receive the least classroom attention. Thus they may be more helpful in developing a general attitude toward language than in furnishing direct pedagogical assistance. Nevertheless, Joos has made a real contribution toward an analysis of the styles of discourse, and has fortified this by listing at least some specific linguistic features characteristic of each. He would be the last to say that the analysis could not be carried beyond the point that he has taken it.

As a concluding note, it is important to note the manner in which these changing views of the levels of language are reflected in *Webster's Third New International Dictionary*. This is to be seen primarily in one omission and in one new distinction.

The omission is the label *colloquial*. This was discarded, according to the editors, on the ground that "it is impossible to know whether a word out of context is colloquial or not."[11] It may well be that the constant misinterpretation of the term, referred to earlier, also had something to do with the decision of the editors. We must remember, however, that despite the omission of the label, the stated aim of the dictionary is "coverage of the current vocabulary of standard written and spoken English."[12] It is reasonable to conclude, therefore, that in the light of a virtual fourfold increase in the number of citations upon which this dictionary is based, over the preceding one, the editors have delegated to the dictionary user the responsibility of judging the context in which a word occurs, an editorial shift of responsibility which has met with a certain amount of criticism.

The new distinction to be found in Webster III is that between *substandard* and *nonstandard*. The first of these is defined as "conforming to a pattern of linguistic usage that exists throughout the American language community but differs in choice of word or word form from that of the prestige group in that community."[13] *Drownded* and *hisself* may be taken as examples of such substandard forms.

The label *nonstandard* is applied to a very small number of words which can scarcely stand without some status label but which nevertheless are too widely current in reputable context to be labelled *substandard*.[14] *Irregardless* is one of those so marked. Whether or not the ascription of this particular word is accurate is beside the point. What we seem to have here is a new distinction between a nonprestigious feature which occurs only in the language of substandard speakers and one which is shared by the two levels, standard and substandard. These two labels replace *illiterate,* the term employed in earlier editions and, as has been indicated, no longer literally or strictly applicable to most parts of the English language community. The replacements continue the Kenyon tradition of nonpejorative labels.

In short, what has happened over the years is a clear recognition of the complexity of the language situation in an equally complex culture, and the attendant conclusion that this renders untenable a single hierarchical arrangement of language levels. We have come to see that class dialect, the nature of the medium, the features of the style all enter into the situation, that they interlock and intersect. The result has been an abandonment of the notion that an individual word or form can be pinpointed on an ascending scale without reference to its total context.

Pedagogically this places a greater burden upon the teacher. What he must try to develop in his students is a highly sensitive feeling for language, an instinct for a situation and the language appropriate to it. And of course he cannot escape the necessity of first developing this sensitivity within himself. Finally, what the linguistic profession must do is to pursue still further some of the fruitful suggestions which have emanated from the work of the last fifteen years.

Four

USAGE:

FINDING AND INTERPRETING

THE FACTS

IN THE PRECEDING CHAPTER WE SAW HOW THE CONCEPT OF English usage had changed over the past fifty years, from a simple right-or-wrong dichotomy to something infinitely more complex. Today we normally take into consideration the situation and style of the discourse, the nature of the medium (speech or writing), as well as the social level to which the particular word or construction may properly be ascribed. The concluding recommendation was that teachers needed to make their students sensitive to these matters, and that in so doing, it was imperative that they develop a similar, or even greater, sensitivity within themselves.

Everyone will concede, I believe, that this is reasonably sound advice even though it is by no means original or startling in nature. But, like so much advice that flows from well-insulated collegiate circles to teachers, exposed every hour of every school day to the realities and practical exigencies of the elementary-school and secondary-school classroom, it falls far short of being concrete and truly helpful. It is all very well to recommend the development of a sensitivity to stylistic nuances, to complex language situations, and to the status of specific usage items in each of these, but this merely raises a further question, "How do we go about it?" It is the purpose of this chapter to furnish some concrete answers to the last of these questions, that of current usage.

There are some 260,000,000 speakers of English as a first or native language, scattered over five continents of the globe. Thus the totality of language activity which goes on even at any one moment is so vast as to literally stagger the imagination. How many sentences are being spoken and written in English as you read these particular lines? How many are spoken and written in the course of just one day?

Such questions are of value only in making the point that the accumulated linguistic experience of any one native speaker of English constitutes a very small, almost an infinitesimal, portion of what we may call the current totality of the language. Moreover, there is the very great likelihood that it is a highly skewed rather than a representative sample.

On this latter point, I can speak from personal experience. Despite the fact that I have been using the English language for more than half a century, I seem to learn something about it almost every day. A casual but fairly regular reading of the Bloomington (Indiana) *Daily Herald Telephone* at the time that this particular chapter was being written added the terms *bush-hogging* and *mammy bench* to my vocabulary. These happened to be lexical items; I could quite as easily have encountered a variation in inflectional form, in the structure of a verb phrase, or in the use of a preposition that was not a part of my idiolect. I can only assume that what is true of me is true to some extent of most English teachers: their experience with the language is too limited to permit them to rely upon their intuition or *Sprach-*

gefühl as a reliable criterion for all of the linguistic judgments which they are called upon to make in the course of their day-to-day professional activities.

If individual intuition is inadequate to the task at hand, the obvious recourse is to sources of information about the English language which represent the collective industry and experience of those who have made it their business to gather the facts of English on a large scale, and who have developed techniques for presenting them in a systematic and organized fashion. In short, dictionaries, linguistic atlases, compendia of usage, and scholarly grammars are important tools of the English-teaching profession. Teachers cannot get along without them, nor should they try. But unless they know how to consult them and how to interpret the information which is to be found in them, they may well be doing themselves and their pupils a disservice. Incorrect information with respect to language can sometimes do more harm than no information. And to the extent that these sources of information are the products of careful scholarship, reflecting procedures both of collecting and of editing which are in keeping with sound linguistic concepts, to this extent the science of language makes its contribution to the almost infinite number of judgments which teachers must regularly make about the language of their students, in oral as well as in written discourse.

It is convenient to begin with dictionaries. They are of primary importance anyway, but the heated and often unilluminating debate of the past few years over the attitude and editorial procedures of *Webster's Third New International Dictionary* has tended to confuse a great many teachers about the extent and nature of its resources and the uses to which they may be put. I am assuming here that although abridged desk dictionaries, many of which have not been sufficiently reduced in size, are adequate for student use, the great unabridged dictionaries, including the Webster, the *Century*, the Funk and Wagnalls *Standard* and of course the *Oxford* are indispensable as professional equipment for the teacher. It is not likely that he will own more than one of them, but he should have recourse to all of them.

There is no need to enter into the controversy concerning the Webster III except to use it as an object lesson to demonstrate a cardinal point: most people in this country, teachers included, do not really know how to use a dictionary to its fullest advantage. They are unaware of its editorial principles. They fail to interpret properly the information that it has to offer. As a consequence, misconceptions arise and misinformation is all too easily disseminated. For example, as a consequence of some carelessly written promotional material, some hasty reading on the part of a linguistically unsophisticated book-reviewer, and one or two other equally accidental and irrelevant factors, descriptive or structural linguistics has been held responsible for the failure of this dictionary to satisfy a widespread public demand for authoritarian judgment. Actually, except for a quasi-phonemic notation in its pronunciation key and the presence of one or two competent linguists on its consulting and editorial staffs, any connection between structural linguistics and the current Merriam product exists chiefly in the imaginations of Jacques Barzun and Dwight McDonald.

What has generally been overlooked in this connection is that Webster III reflects no change in lexicographic or editorial principle, broadly speaking, from its predecessor, the second edition of 1934, which was already firmly committed to an accurate presentation of linguistic fact, to the extent to which this lay in its power, rather than to the exercise of an authoritarian function. Thus the title of such an article as Wilson Follett's "Sabotage in Springfield"[1] reveals an utter lack of comprehension of the editorial principles of both editions. Where the third edition does differ from the second is in the degree to which these principles are logically and consistently carried out. In short, it indicates a failure on Follett's part to read the dictionary prefaces, a weakness which he shares with the majority of those who consult dictionaries. However, as a professional dealing with language, the English teacher can scarcely afford to be numbered among this group.

Distressing as it is to find that the dictionary prefaces belong to the vast no man's land of what is carefully composed and printed, but not read, it is even more distressing to discover that the individual entries themselves are read with much less care and precision than they merit. It would scarcely be feasible here to point out all of the features of a dictionary entry which should command the attention of a careful reader and to warn against all of the possibilities of misinterpretation. This should be part of the professional preparation of every high-school teacher of English and every teacher of the language arts in the elementary school.

We shall find it useful, however, to take up just two specific points of criticism which have been leveled at Webster III, simply as illustrations of the failure to read carefully and of the tendency to jump at conclusions without considering all of the evidence. The first has to do with *ain't,* that perennial *bête noir* of the linguistically squeamish. To begin with, several feature writers for newspapers and magazines made a great point of discovering that the word was actually included among the entries in the new dictionary and announced it with an air somewhat akin to having apprehended Noah Webster *in flagrante delicto.*

Now what are the facts? Of course it is in Webster III, as it had been in Webster II, in the *Oxford English Dictionary,* and in innumerable others over the past century. Apparently the mistaken premise upon which the journalists operated was that any substandard locution was not really a word and therefore did not merit inclusion in a reputable dictionary. Some of them at least were undoubtedly so stunned to find it in the most recent edition that the obvious procedure of checking its inclusion in earlier ones did not occur to them, and besides, they may well have been in a hurry to get a newsworthy article written.

Those who did take the trouble to read the entry were offended by the lack of a blanket condemnation of the word, and this added further fuel to the fire. Now, what does Webster III really say about *ain't*? Actually the treatment is very careful; no lexicographer in his right mind could afford to be anything else here. The entry is divided into two parts: *ain't* as a contraction of *am, are,* and *is,* with *not* constitutes the first portion. The second deals with *ain't* as a contraction of *have* and *has* plus *not.* This latter is labeled substandard, which should satisfy everyone except those who, through some twisted logic, would maintain that the word should not be included in the dictionary at all.

With respect to *ain't* as a contraction of various forms of *be* plus *not,* there is the following comment: "Though disapproved by many and more common in less educated speech, used orally in most parts of the U.S. by many cultivated speakers, especially in the phrase 'ain't I.'" Though clearly objectionable from the point of view of someone who expected the editors to give the form summary dismissal as a vulgarism, the statement is carefully framed and cautiously qualified. It reveals an attitude of widespread disapproval of the form. It points to a considerable amount of cultivated use despite the disapproval and suggests that this is fairly general throughout the country. It records an even wider use among the less educated. It recognizes the first person, negative interrogative as the form with the highest incidence of cultivated use. It is true that varying emphases might have been given to the four components of this particular statement, and in fact a revision of this nature has been suggested by Sheridan Baker.[2] The important point, however, is that the Webster editors appear to have attempted, in all good conscience, a careful summary of a complex language situation.

Although someone might have developed a statement as discriminating and as carefully qualified as this out of whole cloth, the chances are that it has its origin in some body of collected data. Actually, there is a close correspondence between the Webster statement and that which appears in E. Bagby Atwood's *Survey of Verb Forms in the Eastern United States*.[3] Atwood's work is a summary of the information on verb morphology contained in *The Linguistic Atlas of New England* and the unpublished materials of the linguistic atlases of the Middle Atlantic and the South American states. In treating this particular item, he, too, points out that *ain't I* along with certain other contractions shows "a surprising degree of currency in the cultivated group," even to the point of predominance in certain areas. He estimated that nearly one-third of the cultured informants in the Middle and South Atlantic states used *ain't I,* and a little less than one-fourth of those in New England, most of them perhaps as an alternate to other forms. All told, this conclusion was based upon evidence furnished by well over 1,200 informants, 141 of whom were selected as representative of cultivated speech. True enough, Atwood's study covered only the eastern seaboard, and we are not yet certain whether his conclusions would apply with equal validity to the rest of the country. In fact, all of the data are by no means in hand at the present time.

I hold no particular brief for *ain't* as a verb contraction; in fact, I do not use it myself except in jocular fashion. At the same time, it is quite apparent to me why it persists in the first person, negative interrogation, to the degree that it does. But the fact that in the course of the entire welter of controversy over the Webster III treatment of this particular item, Atwood's findings have become a matter of discussion only recently, points to an appalling lack of familiarity with one of the primary collections of information about American English.

A little more than a year ago, after I had spoken somewhat wearily and disparagingly about the quality of the criticism of Webster III, a distinguished scholar took me to task for defending a dictionary which would condone the use of *disinterested* in the sense of "uninterested" rather than "impartial." Again his judgment had been formed only on the basis of what is to be found in Webster III. What he did not know was that the order of definitions in Webster III, Webster II, and the *Oxford English Dictionary* is identical. All of them place the meaning "uninterested" before the meaning "impartial" because it happens to be the earliest one recorded in English, and they are all committed by editorial policy to a chronological ordering of their definitions. Moreover, Webster II had no restrictive label on the term; it did not condemn it as loose, improper, or illiterate. The *Oxford English Dictionary* contents itself with questioning whether or not the earlier meaning might now be obsolete. Actually, if one takes the trouble to consult the Webster III synonymy for this word, given in connection with the adjective *indifferent,* he will discover that some people do object to this use of *disinterested,* a fact not recorded in either of the other dictionaries.

It is true, as I have said previously, that Webster III places a greater responsibility upon the person who uses it than does its predecessors. But this is the case with citation dictionaries generally, notably the Oxford. Any teacher who uses them must get into the habit of reading the citations as a check on the usage labels and at times even on the meanings ascribed to the entry-words. At times it is even helpful to consult the bibliography, when there is one, for further hints about the works from which the citations have been taken. It is important, moreover, that every teacher be acquainted with the *Dictionary of American English*[4] and the *Dictionary of Americanisms,*[5] and that he have a clear understanding of the differences in scope and coverage between the two.

Even with respect to the various abridged dictionaries which are available for classroom use, the teacher should be able to identify the differences in editorial policy which characterize them. There are minor variations in the pronunciation keys, in the kind and amount of grammatical information that is given, in the handling of etymology. Some arrange their definitions in chronological order, others on the basis of frequency. Some are supported by collections of citations in the editorial offices; others decidedly less so. Certainly their application of status and usage labels is far from uniform. There is often as much to be learned from the differences in their treatments of a word as from their similarities. In short, the dictionary is an important tool, and just as a carpenter learns to distinguish various types and makes of hammers and saws, recognizing particular virtues and adaptability to specific uses in each, so must the teacher come to regard his shelf of dictionaries.

The various linguistic atlas projects have already been mentioned as a source of first-hand data on the English language. Each of them is careful to differentiate current usage on three social levels, ranging from those speakers of the language with minimal education to those who were selected as specimens of cultivated speech. They deal primarily with the features of vocabulary, pronunciation, inflectional forms, and syntax which differ regionally throughout the country. Although of the seven or eight regional atlases for which materials have been collected, only the *Linguistic Atlas of New England*[6] has been published, and even this is not available everywhere. There are, however, three volumes which summarize the atlas findings for the entire eastern seaboard, Kurath's *Word Geography of the Eastern United States,*[7] Kurath and McDavid's *Pronunciation of English in the Atlantic States,*[8] and Atwood's *A Survey of Verb Forms in the Eastern United States,* to which I have already referred.

These three summary volumes are useful in that they will indicate the differences, in at least part of the country, between folk speech and the standard language. A glance at just one of the maps in Atwood will show the teacher that south of the border between Pennsylvania and Maryland there is likely to be a strong tendency on the part of children coming from homes where the standard language is not spoken to use either *taken* or *tuck* as the past tense of *take,* whereas in Pennsylvania, New Jersey, New York, and New England this is simply not a problem for children born in the area. Conversely, if the teacher is convinced that *hadn't ought* is a form which should be eliminated, it is New York, New Jersey, and New England where difficulties will arise, but generally not in southern Pennsylvania, Maryland, Delaware and the South Atlantic states. When the materials for the North Central states become available, it will be clearly evident that the teacher who objects to *sick to his stomach* will have to work hard to eliminate it in Michigan and Wisconsin, but will have little trouble in Indiana, southern Ohio, and southern Illinois. The regional distribution of folk-speech forms does have an important bearing on the inclusion of particular items in the curriculum; consequently, it is to the advantage of every English teacher to be able to use and interpret the most authoritative sources of information on regional differences within the United States.

In addition there are a number of manuals of current usage which, taken together, form a valuable part of the English teacher's tool kit. Among the most important of these are Bryant, *Current American Usage;*[9] Evans, *A Dictionary of Contemporary American Usage;*[10] Fowler, *Modern English Usage;*[11] Horwill, *Dictionary of Modern American Usage;*[12] and Nicholson, *American English Usage.*[13] Each of these differs somewhat from the others in coverage, general attitudes, and the nature of the source material upon which it is based.

Fowler purports to base his conclusions upon the citation slips collected for the *Oxford English Dictionary* and in fact does quote the OED frequently, but he is quite likely to go off on his own when the evidence does not point to what he considers to be the proper conclusions. An excellent example of this is to be found in his treatment of the word *flamboyant,* which, as he correctly explains, "is a word borrowed from writers on architecture who apply it to the French style . . . characterized by tracings whose wavy lines suggest the shape or motion of tongues of flame. It is now fashionable in transferred senses; but whereas it should be synonymous with *flowing* or *flexible* or *sinuous* or *free,* it is more often made to mean *florid* or *showy* or *vividly coloured* or *courting publicity.* A word of which the true and usual meanings are at odds and could well be spared."[14]

Two significant points emerge in the treatment of this term. First, a distinction is drawn between the "true" and the "usual" meanings of a word. True must, of course, be equated with etymological, but obviously there are limits to the degree to which the etymological meaning of a word can be insisted upon. No one in his right mind could insist that *nice* be used in the sense of "ignorant" or that *dilapidated* be applied only to stone structures. Second, it is quite evident that the social status or cultivation of the user does not influence Fowler's judgment, once he has arrived at a decision. Two of the OED citations for the so-called loose or usual uses of *flamboyant* were drawn from the writings of Edward Dowden and George Saintsbury, both distinguished literary critics and scholars. It would be unfair to Fowler, however, to conclude on this negative note. The book does have its charm. It contains much information that is eminently useful, and even when Fowler denies facts and history, he is often witty and entertaining in doing so. But it is well to check his judgments against the factual record. It is clearly a tribute to Fowler that his work has been adapted twice in the last three decades and that a new edition has just appeared.

In 1935 H. W. Horwill compiled a handbook of *Modern American Usage*. Having lived both in England and in the United States, he was keenly aware of the differences in English as it is spoken on the two sides of the Atlantic Ocean. His compilation was not, as he said, intended "to teach Americans how to write or speak American." He includes only words which are common to the vocabularies of both England and the United States but which have different meanings or uses on the two sides of the Atlantic. As such, it is very valuable to Americans as well, except that the words are entered in their American rather than their English form. Therefore, unless an American knows that his own use differs from British, and this is not always likely, he will scarcely be moved to seek an English equivalent under the American entry. Horwill is very scrupulous in always giving American citations to support the meanings which he includes. It is a well-documented work and unquestionably deserves to be brought up to date.

In 1957, more than thirty years after the appearance of Fowler, the Oxford University Press published what is described as "a simplified MEU, with American variations, retaining as much of the original as space allowed." Margaret Nicholson was the compiler. Her work was entitled *A Dictionary of American English Usage*. It sought to recognize the new words and idioms which have come into the language during the past three decades; this edition conceded also that there were forms of speech and writing characteristic of the United States which Fowler had not recorded, and she attempted to include them. Where Fowler had no entry at all for *fortnight,* Miss Nicholson comments that the word "is more at home in England than in the U.S. and often sounds self-conscious in American speech." Where Fowler concerned himself only with the spelling of the verb *to chisel,* Nicholson adds the slang meaning 'to cheat.' She points out that in the United States one resigns from an office whereas in England "he resigned his office" may be encountered. Fowler's uncertainty as to whether *mugwump* and *highbrow* are alike in meaning is replaced by a straightforward treatment of the first of these words. All told the book has its useful qualities but it remains a rather strange combination of the intensely personal touch that Fowler gave to many of his judgments and the somewhat more objective air of more recent ventures into American lexicography and usage.

That Nicholson continues to enjoy a degree of popularity is due in part to the less prescriptive and somewhat more liberal attitudes of the remaining two manuals. The earlier of these, *A Dictionary of Contemporary American Usage* by Bergen Evans and Cornelia L. Evans appeared in the same year as Miss Nicholson's adaptation of Fowler. The particular objects of the Evans' concern are the people who speak well but who are paralyzed with uncertainty over grammatical matters when they try to write. He reassures them by pointing out that language changes constantly, decade by decade. He goes on:

> Since language changes this much, no one can say how a word "ought" to be used. The best that anyone can say is how it *is* being used, and this is what grammar should tell us. It should give us information on what is currently accepted as good En-

glish, bringing together as many details as possible in a few general rules or principles, so that it will be easier for us to remember them.[15]

Good English is defined as "the kind of English that is used by the most respected people, the sort of English that will make readers or listeners regard you as an educated person."[16] He also takes the position that "modern usage encourages informality wherever possible and reserves formality for very few occasions." He employs as sources of information the *Oxford English Dictionary,* the *Dictionary of American English,* the *Dictionary of Americanisms,* the work of such grammarians as Charles C. Fries and Otto Jespersen, and articles on specific items of usage which have appeared in the journal *American Speech.*[17] In short, he uses a fairly wide range of factual data and interprets them liberally. His comment on *like* will serve, not unfairly I believe, as an index of his treatment of disputed usages:

> The modern purist claims that *like* is correctly used as a preposition and carries the meaning of *like to,* and incorrectly used where it functions as a conjunction and carries the meaning *like as.* There is no doubt but that *like* is accepted as a conjunction in the United States today and that there is excellent literary tradition for this. There is no reason why anyone should take the trouble to learn when *like* is a conjunction and when it is a preposition, unless he wants to. But if anyone wants to be a purist, he should be a thorough one. He should not himself use *like* as a conjunction in some constructions and condemn other people for using it in this way in other constructions.[18]

Much the same attitude and approach characterize Margaret M. Bryant's *Current American Usage,* a work which had its inception as a project of the Committee on Current English Usage of the National Council of Teachers of English. There are two major differences between her work and that of the Evanses.

Miss Bryant limited herself to 240 entries, but many of these are grammatical points which cover under a single heading a number of specific items which might be treated individually in another manual. Thus the entry for *get* includes such various matters as *gotten* as past participle, *have got* in the various senses of possession and obligation, *get* to indicate the inception of an action, *get* and *got* as passive auxiliaries.

Of all of the usage manuals this has the most complete documentation of the data. Every item is supported with references to citation dictionary treatments, the summary studies of the Linguistic Atlas findings, special articles in various professional journals, scholarly grammars of English, and special studies made at the request of the author. A detailed bibliography of usage studies is one of a number of helpful appendices.

One study of usage quite different from the others deserves special mention. In the early 1930's S. A. Leonard, following up an earlier collaborative study with H. Y. Moffett, undertook a survey for the National Council of Teachers of English, which, when it appeared in published form, was entitled *Current English Usage*.[19] It differs from the manuals already described in that, despite its title, it is really a survey of opinion about usage rather than a survey of usage itself. The monograph reports the judgments of well over 200 authors, editors, businessmen, teachers of English, teachers of speech, and linguists (both British and American) as to the relative acceptability of some 230 specific items of usage which at that time were often condemned as incorrect in school textbooks but which were, at the same time, common in actual use.

Though clearly lacking in authority as a sampling of actual usage, the study is of value as an indication of attitudes toward usage, at least toward the items which were included, on the part of various groups. The results reported on the use of *awfully* as an intensive (*This room is awfully cold*) show the extent to which opinions can differ. Of 30 linguists reporting, one felt it acceptable for formal use, 29 for informal, and no one condemned it as illiterate. Members of the Modern Language Association were almost as tolerant. Their ratings were: 2, acceptable for formal use; 59, acceptable informally; 3, illiterate. This was in striking contrast to their colleagues in the high-school classrooms; of 51 members of the National Council of Teachers of English, 10 stigmatized it as illiterate, and the proportion of speech teachers who condemned it was even higher. Authors and businessmen disliked it to about the same degree, whereas editors were somewhat more willing to accept the term. The final judgment on the item was "established" particularly for informal use, with the comment, "It probably belongs among those expressions which are emerging from slang into the lighter levels of cultivated speech, and is certainly not worth trying to eliminate from the speech of school children."[20]

The study has further value for distinguishing between different instances or examples of the same syntactic construction. For example, there appears to be somewhat less of an insistence on the use of the genitive of a proper noun as the subject of a gerund (What was the reason for Bennett making that disturbance?) than when the subject is a pronoun (What are the chances of them being found?). The first of these constructions was rated acceptable as cited; the second disputable. Much of the value of this monograph resides in the tabulations of the ratings, but like a dictionary preface, this part of the work is rarely consulted. Another noteworthy feature is the punctuation study, which constitutes the first portion of the work. This is a survey not of opinion but of actual practice as reported by the editors of books, magazines, and newspapers respectively, about 150 all told. There is much to be learned from a close and thoughtful observation of the differences in the practice of these three groups.

A final source of information on usage consists of scholarly treatments of English grammar, designed for the professional student of language rather than the layman. A few of these have already been mentioned: Jespersen's eight-volume *Modern English Grammar* and George O. Curme's two works, entitled *Syntax* and *Parts of Speech and Accidence*. There are others, including H. Poutsma, *A Grammar of Late Modern English,* H. Kruisinga, *Handbook of Present Day English,* R. W. Zandvoort, *Handbook of English Grammar,* all careful studies of the language by foreign scholars. These books are of particular value in that they, like the scholarly dictionaries, fortify their observations about matters of English form and syntax by numerous quotations from actual English usage, present and past. Thus, in treating the use of a plural verb with *none* as subject, Jespersen cites More, Shakespeare, Goldsmith, Johnson, Scott, one of the Brontës, Morris, Shaw, Stevenson, and Kipling, giving several instances from some of the authors.[21] This, of course, is more informative and of far greater value than a dozen textbook pronouncements without supporting evidence. Curme's *Syntax* has three pages illustrating the connectives used with causal clauses,[22] again ranging from Caxton and Sidney to Sheila Kaye-Smith.

Charles C. Fries's *American English Grammar*[23] is also fortified by illustrative citations, but of a somewhat different kind. Fries selected as the corpus of his study some 3,000 letters in the files of what was then the Bureau of Education, Department of the Interior, of the United States government. Information as to the place of birth, age, education, and occupational history of each of the writers was also available. On the basis especially of the education and occupation of the writers, the letters were sorted into three groups, representing the illiterate, the users of common English, and the users of socially acceptable or Standard

English. Fries was thus able to describe the forms and syntax of American English on three levels, making liberal use of citations and quantitative data in presenting his conclusions. With respect to one of the problems which was discussed briefly in the foregoing description of the Leonard study, namely, the use of the genitive of the noun preceding the gerund, Fries has thirteen uninflected forms and only one that is inflected, leading him to the conclusion that "the inflected form of nouns is *not* the normal practice before gerunds in Standard English."[24]

The chief purpose of this chapter has been to demonstrate that there is literally a wealth of material on usage, most of it readily available to the teacher. In fact, in the interests of space I have omitted any mention of pronouncing dictionaries, dialect dictionaries, dictionaries of slang, and a number of interesting special studies on grammar. Teachers are constantly called upon, in one way or another, to make judgments and come to decisions on matters of usage, and there are many occasions when school textbooks are not adequate to the purpose. Then it becomes a matter of using the kinds of source materials which have been mentioned here, and even more important, of interpreting them intelligently. Linguistic scholarship has placed in the hands of the teacher the tools with which these tasks may be accomplished. It is the teacher's responsibility to use them well.

Five

LINGUISTICS
AND THE TEACHING
OF COMPOSITION

At this point in the development of our broad topic, namely, the potential contributions of linguistics to the teaching of English, we move into areas where the systematic study of language is cast in the role of an auxiliary rather than a principal factor. As long as we were concerned with such matters as the various approaches to grammar, varieties and styles of language, and the interpretation of factual data on usage, we were wholly in the realm of linguistics, and the basic considerations were the quality of the approach, the soundness of the method, and the accuracy of the data. As we come to deal with composition, literature, and reading, we shall see that language, though important, is not always the sole factor, and we must be prepared to see this reflected in the size and nature of the part that linguistics plays.

With respect to the topic of this particular chapter, we may best begin by asking ourselves why we teach composition at all. If we come at the question from a narrow point of view, our answer will undoubtedly be phrased in terms of a service concept:

the student must know how to express himself cogently and articulately in order to perform effectively in the rest of his school subjects, to write papers and reports, to take examinations, and so on. I would prefer, however, to take a somewhat broader approach here and to say that a higher literacy, or perhaps more accurately, a higher articulateness is an essential ingredient of a general or liberal education. If our social order is to continue over the next three or four decades in a form which we can approve, presumably one in which wise and sound policies concerning all aspects of life will emerge from public debate that is at once vigorous and incisive, the need for skill in the use of language will be greater than it has ever been before. We shall need more individuals who can express themselves cogently and think clearly, and at the same time, the quality of the thinking and the expression must improve.

I do not believe that we are likely to see in the future any profound differences in the way in which this skill will be developed. We shall continue to depend in the main upon guided practice in writing. We shall continue to assume that the more a student writes, the greater fluency and facility he will develop, and that continued insistence upon logical organization and precision of expression will result in improvement with respect to those qualities. Such recent developments as the use of lay readers and team teaching do not alter the basic pedagogical strategy; they merely provide mechanisms for implementing it more effectively. Where then, does linguistics function? What sort of place has it in composition teaching?

Let me hasten to say that I reject completely the concept of a "linguistic method" of teaching composition. In fact, the term frightens me, for I fear that it may lead many to expect from linguistics a miraculous set of results which the discipline and its practitioners are wholly unprepared and cannot be expected to produce. This will be evident, I believe, if we simply review the various tasks which the composition teacher must perform.

Certainly, a major problem in the teaching of composition is that of motivation. So long as groups of twenty-five students, as part of an automatically scheduled activity, address a weekly communication of definitely specified word length to the harassed individual on the other side of the desk, on a topic which has been chosen for them rather than something which springs from a natural urge to communicate, so long will theme writing remain a palpably artificial situation. Motivation is one of the major problems of a writing course. How does one get his students to the point where they are bursting to communicate, to the point where they can scarcely contain themselves, and their fingers itch for a pen? I don't know the answer; I doubt that anyone else knows more than a small part of it. I must confess that I see little or nothing in linguistics that bears at all directly on the problem.

Some teachers, acting on the assumption that language is the most appropriate content for the writing course, do manage from time to time to create a stir of interest over moot questions of usage. Others try to warm over the rapidly cooling debate about dictionaries occasioned by the appearance of Webster III. Dialects can, at times, generate a certain amount of curiosity and concern. But these devices work only on occasion and usually only for a limited period.

Motivation will receive a decided assist from theme topics that are fresh, exciting, and stimulating, but which also remain within the student's realm of competence, within his potential sphere of imagination as well as his actual experience. The teacher has a right to expect a degree of originality from at least some of his students. But in general, it takes ingenuity behind the teacher's desk to breed originality in front of it. A teacher who assigns as a theme topic, "How I Spent My Vacation," deserves just what he is going to get—a series of papers in which the students tell him how they spent their vacations. Originality is one of the qualities upon which we place a premium in student writing, yet save within rather definitely circumscribed limits, we cannot expect linguistics to breed a joy in playing with ideas.

For the most part, what we look for in our student themes are evidences of tight logical organization and direct movement toward a specifically stated goal. This is largely because of the emphasis, in college composition classes at least, upon expository and argumentative writing—an emphasis justified on utilitarian grounds. In this connection it has been claimed that the structural analysis of the written sentence, with its concern for the placement of modifiers, for clarity of pronoun references to their antecedents, with its potential for discovering ambiguities, breeds a concern for logic and for organization, which in turn can be transferred to such larger units of discourse as the paragraph and indeed the composition as a whole. This is possible, given a workable approach to the structure of the written sentence and the kind of imaginative teaching that will take advantage of every opportunity to demonstrate the applicability of structural principles to the larger linguistic units. Whether any considerable number of teachers can make it work is an open question. At least here is one area where linguistics has a potential contribution to make, although it must be recognized that except for Zellig Harris' discourse analysis, little thought has been given to units or stretches of language longer than the sentence. Recently Francis Christensen has devoted some attention to what he has called the generative rhetoric of the paragraph, which is an extension of the techniques of the transformational grammarians.

We must recognize also that themes consist not only of sentences but of the words used in them. Good writing poses problems of diction. Up to the present, linguists have given very little attention to this aspect of language. Diction has been left, more or less, to the semanticists and the students of stylistics. Again the conclusion is obvious—linguistics will not identify the tired phrase, the worn out cliché, the overwritten sentence in a way that is helpful to the composition instructor, nor will it guide the student to the refreshing, the supremely right word, phrase, or metaphor.

None of these disclaimers should be interpreted as a criticism of linguistics as a discipline or as an opposition to the inclusion of the systematic study of language at one or more points in the school curriculum—when it is studied as a topic of interest in its own right. I repeat that I am merely being cautious, overcautious in fact, in making claims for linguistics as an easy answer to any and all of the English teacher's problems. There was a time when the existence of linguistics was too much ignored by the English-teaching profession, and there were, indeed, some who were actively hostile to it, since it appeared to them to suggest a denial of humanistic values.

At present the danger seems to come from the opposite direction. Although some hostility to linguistics continues, it also shares the aura of the exciting and the unexplored which surrounds the newer mathematics and physics. As I have already indicated, there is loose talk of "linguistic methods" of teaching reading, composition, and the foreign languages, and of course, there aren't any. There can be linguistically based materials in some of these areas, there can be linguistically oriented approaches to certain parts of the teaching of these subjects, but that is about all. Those who have the best interests of the discipline at heart do not want to see linguistics oversold. We must not lead teachers to expect from it miracles that it is not in a position to perform.

It may be profitable to approach the teaching of composition from another angle, namely by trying to set some realistic limits to what we, as English teachers, may hope to achieve in our lifetimes, taking into consideration the state of the language, the general cultural framework, and the particular teaching situations in which we have to work. I think we should begin by conceding that we shall not produce in this country, in this century, a generation for whom distinguished prose is a natural mode of expression. Nor shall we, in our time, succeed in developing a public whose taste in welcoming good prose and rejecting the bad is almost instinctive, like the German and Italian reaction toward music or the French toward art. There are no school courses, there is little or no school training in these subjects in the countries that I have mentioned. The sensitivity to which I have referred is simply part of a shared common experience, almost an instinct.

As a people, we are essentially lacking in a sense of and an appreciation for style in language. Little wonder, since we have had so little opportunity to experience it. Our great public orators, those with a manner calculated to appeal to the intellect, disappeared from the scene over a century ago. William Jennings Bryan, the one great figure at the close of the century, covered the defects in his logic with sheer emotionalism. In our own time we have had but one articulate public personage, whose ability to use the language rises to the level that I have been talking about, namely, Adlai Stevenson. We have hundreds who are either linguistically insensitive or would perhaps be better off if they were. And the writing that comes from their pens or from those of their ghost-writers is no more distinguished for its quality than the talk which issues from the amplifiers.

Lest this sound entirely negative and pessimistic, I hasten to say that there is a reasonable and realistic minimum which I should like to achieve, and I believe that it is possible. What I hope we might develop, and this would be no small accomplishment if we succeeded in it, is a public taste which will demand of those who address any group of persons, large or small, in speech or in writing, the qualities of directness, economy and clarity. I should like to have us develop a public taste that will be impatient with, possibly even intolerant of, blurred expression, tautology, and faulty logic. I want a public taste which will laugh pretentiousness, jargon, and clichés out of court. Though modest when compared with an instinctive sense of style in prose, this is no small order. It is, indeed, a first step on the way toward a larger goal.

Think of what would happen if we succeeded in this. Think of how many voices would be stilled at the county, state, and national conventions of our political parties. Suppose that candidates for political office were actually afraid to talk nonsense. In the face of a demand for logic, clarity, and economy of expression, think of the change in newspaper editorials, in public utterances from the pulpit and lecture platform. Think of the revolution that a public sensitive to emotionally slanted expression and accustomed to the careful analysis of whatever is said or written might bring about in the so-called professions of public relations and advertising. Surely, it is difficult to maintain that if we succeeded in all this, we would not be better off for it. And I think that success here is not impossible; at the very least it is a defensible and worthwhile aim.

It is so easy to become intrigued with an idea like this that one is likely to put it in unnecessarily negative terms. Certainly, we shall not accomplish this aim by frightening people within an inch of their lives about the language they use. On the contrary, we shall achieve it only by building confidence through carefully guided practice.

I am quite convinced that the form and quality of our public utterances are as bad as they are because the writers, in the main, lack a sense of mastery of the language. Anyone who has served on public bodies knows that the vast majority of his associates are not only reluctant but almost afraid to put pen to paper. It rarely occurs to persons in public life to attempt to clarify an emergent or half-formed idea by writing it out, toying with the sentences, juggling the paragraphs, experimenting with one word after another. Recently I have had occasion to read some reports addressed to some of the highest agencies in government. They read as if they were written by persons with all thumbs. The expression is awkward and stultified, yet professionally the authors are highly capable.

We may well ask, why this reluctance to write, this very real awkwardness in self-expression. Any answer to the question is essentially guesswork, I confess, but I believe that the written medium tends to frighten a good many people out of their wits. Bergen Evans speaks of "the demon that numbs their fingers when they take hold of a pen" and fills them "with paralyzing uncertainty whenever they stop to think." And again why is this? Because so many writers have been so overwhelmed by warnings of what they should not do, born largely of an insufficient understanding of language in its larger and more profound aspects. As a consequence, language has become something which masters, which dominates them instead of the other way around.

Several competent British observers of the American scene tend to corroborate my judgment on this point. Some years ago, Miss Marjorie Daunt, reader in Old English at Birkbeck College, University of London, was in the United States on a lecture tour, speaking on various aspects of the English language. She was accustomed to say that, considered from one point of view, the speakers of any language could be divided into three classes: the assured, the anxious, and the indifferent—a differentiation which bears a rough resemblance to the upper, middle, and lower class stratification of society. She then went on to say that throughout her travels in this country she had come across no one who could be characterized as indifferent, and that the only two assured speakers she had encountered were two old ladies in Charleston, South Carolina. All the rest were, by inference, anxious. Admittedly, this was a judgment based on slight and casual observation, but its general soundness is reinforced by the fact that the assured speakers did represent an old local culture where there is assurance about many kinds of behavior. Consequently, I am inclined to accept her impression about the amount and degree of linguistic anxiety in this country, at least as it appears to someone from a country where there is a vastly greater amount of linguistic assurance. James West, in his community study entitled *Plainville, U.S.A.,* also commented that all but the most "backwoodsy" speakers frequently ridicule and parody the stratum or strata of speech beneath or older than their own, and at the same time feel uncertain about their own usages.

How then do we proceed to work toward even the modest increase in the amount of linguistic competence which we have set as a goal? In the light of what has been said, it would seem to be a matter of attitude first, and of learning and skill development second. We do not teach attitudes directly with any degree of success. They are transmitted rather than taught; one acquires them through osmosis, so to speak. For this reason it is the attitude toward language on the part of teacher and pupil alike which takes on an importance equal to, or even greater than, practice in the skill of using language and technical knowledge about its structure. We must strive to turn out students who have a feeling that the English langage is a medium they can control, not a Procrustean bed into which they must fit, cut, and trim whatever they have to communicate. Since I am so convinced of the prime importance of attitude, I shall pay far more attention to it than to classroom devices or the mechanics of one or another grammatical analysis. And in this connection it is necessary to clear up some misunderstandings resulting from less than perfect communication and understanding between linguists and classroom teachers.

The first of these has to do with the relationship between speech and writing, which has been dealt with in some of the earlier chapters but in a somewhat different manner. Unfortunately, the linguists have sometimes been misunderstood when they used such phrases as "the primacy of the spoken language." This has been interpreted on occasion to betray a lack of interest in writing, hence in literature, hence in the humanities, on the part of the linguists. What the linguist meant was, first of all, that the essence of language structure was more immediately apparent in the spoken language and that most writing systems not only revealed this structure more or less imperfectly, but actually forced certain changes upon the language to compensate for these imperfections. He would support this position by pointing out that whereas language is very old, writing is relatively new, that every person learns to speak before he learns to read and write, that there are hundreds of languages that are spoken but for which no writing system has been developed, whereas by contrast there are no written languages which are not now spoken or have not been spoken. Even in this literate age, and with the Sunday issue of the *New York Times* as bulky as it is, we still speak far more than we write.

What the linguists have not always emphasized sufficiently is that in a highly sophisticated and literate culture, the written language may have a most interesting structure of its own. What they have neglected to study in anywhere nearly the detail that it merits is the relationship between the spoken and written forms of the language. For teachers of English the problem has become even more complicated by the fact that over the years there has been a decided shift in classroom emphasis from a highly formal style of writing to one less rigid and stylized. According to one current textbook, "Semiformal English is the language you will use for most of your college writing." There is no reason to suppose that the situation is different in the secondary school. To many English teachers, this may well seem like the first step down a perilous and giddy slide toward laxity and incoherence; to such persons the linguist's concern with the spoken language is a clear indication of a covenant with the Tempter.

Certainly, then, a clarification of the linguist's method of dealing with the relationship between spoken and written English is in order. Any number of careful studies concerned with various aspects of this relationship ought to be made. Data on the relative incidence of simple, compound, and complex sentence types in the two varieties of the language should be collected. Even in terms of some exploratory work which has been completed, it can be said quite definitely that the written language does not necessarily have a higher proportion of complex sentences. It would be helpful to have similar data on appositive constructions. Comparative studies of the position of modifying elements, particularly adverbs, adverbial phrases, and subordinate clauses should be undertaken. We also need to know how and where parenthetical expressions of various kinds appear in the two forms of English. We need, in addition, to clarify the relationship between punctuation and the suprasegmental features of intonation, stress, and juncture. Henry Bradley barely began an investigation of this vast subject about forty years ago, and no one has followed it up in systematic fashion.

The answers to the questions I have posed would have a dual utility. In the first place, they would show what structural devices must be employed in writing as compensation for the lack of a systematic notation of stress, intonation, and juncture. In addition, they would serve to suggest something of the stylistic potential of the written language. If information of this nature were to be considered along with data on the development of the student's ability to employ constantly expanding structural patterns, we would be much closer than we are now to the establishment of a pedagogical strategy. Nevertheless, though much work needs to be done, this approach has important implications for the attitudes toward language on the part of both teacher and student. If the relationship between speech and writing can be presented in a framework of logic and reason we are that much closer to overcoming the long-standing fear of the pen.

Another point concerning which the linguists have not been wholly convincing to their English-teaching colleagues concerns the linguistic development of the child. The following quotation from Charles F. Hockett's *Introduction to Modern Linguistics* is fairly typical of the kind of assertion often made by linguists. "By the age of four to six, the normal child is a linguistic adult. He controls, with marginal exceptions if any, the phonemic system of the language; he handles effortlessly the grammatical core; he knows and uses the basic contentive vocabulary of the language."[1]

True enough, Hockett does go on to say that, "he may get tangled in trying to produce longer discourses, as in describing the activities of a morning at school, but clarity in extended exposition is a point on which older people also vary greatly."

Hockett may well be correct in this, but clarity in extended exposition happens to be the principal aim of most composition teaching, and in the light of this, the linguist's claim that a child of six has a grasp of all the fundamental language patterns is quite beside the point as far as the teacher of composition is concerned.

In justice to the linguists, it should be pointed out that they had some valid reasons for their insistence upon early language mastery. They wanted to point out to foreign-language teachers that language learning goes on long before the child is in school, that it proceeds by trial and error and the mastery of patterns, and that it bears little or no relationship to paradigmatic or deductive learning. It also served as a corrective to those teachers who confused the teaching of reading with the learning of language, who were inclined to think that the only thing that mattered in school readers was a vocabulary count, and who must have thought that seven-year-old children actually did talk like the Dick and Jane books.

But what can we believe about the extent to which a child of five or six has mastered the language, and how will this influence the matter of attitude which has been emphasized throughout this chapter? To begin with, it is the mastery of the spoken language to which the linguists refer in statements such as the one which has been quoted. By the time the child enters school, he will have mastered the phonological system just about in its entirety. There are always some few cases of lisping or difficulty with one sound or another. Often these clear up by themselves, and at the risk of being considered a heretic, I shall say that a little knowledge of phonetics on the part of more classroom teachers would make it unnecessary to call in the speech correctionist quite as often as we are prone to.

The child at this stage has mastered the regular inflectional patterns of the language: noun plurals, noun genitives, verb past tenses, and the personal pronouns, if they can be called regular. His principal errors consist of extending the regular patterns analogically to the few irregular nouns and verbs that remain and in confusing the inflectional with the periphrastic comparison of adjectives.

After all is said and done, however, English is primarily a word-order language, and certainly the first-grader has mastered the subject-verb-object order, the modifier-substantive order, inversion of subject and verb to indicate a question, and the mechanics of negation. Simple adverbial placement will pose no problems. If this is the case, what is there left to teach him? The answer is reasonably clear, I believe. Expansion of the basic patterns into complex structures, some control of excessive coordination (we don't want him to connect all of his clauses with *and*), ways of enriching the minimal amount of information that he is likely to content himself with conveying under certain circumstances, especially in a schoolroom environment. Once we have properly clarified the matter, there is no question about the remarkable degree of language control that the first-grader already has, but what this should do is to stimulate our imaginations as to the increase in this mastery that we ought to be able to achieve in the next twelve years.

For this very reason, we need to know much more than we do about the child's linguistic development after the age of six. For example, what are the facts about increase of sentence length? Is there a clearly marked stage when he frequently uses compound sentences before he has mastered patterns of subordination?[2] In what constructions do pupils at various age levels use relative pronouns? When does apposition emerge as a structural device? If the linguist continues to insist that the kindergartener's achievement constitutes mastery of the fundamental language patterns, what the composition teacher will want to know is how these patterns are developed and expanded, and what can be done to facilitate such expansion. Surely this must be capable of description.

Part of the difficulty here lies in the fact that the classic studies of the development of language in children, especially those by Piaget, Gregoire, and the Sterns deal with language at an early age. Even more recently we have had an excellent study on language in the crib.[3] All of this is important and informative, but from the point of view of possible application to the problems of the English classroom such studies need to be extended in scope so as to include all of the operational mechanisms of the language and in range to cover at least the early adolescent years. I set this upper limit because I believe that it is somewhere between the fifth and seventh grades that children do begin to develop something of a written style, a point at which their compositions and their conversation begin to differ.

Another important attitude centers about the question of linguistic continuity. How is a language passed on from one generation to another? The answer is simple: orally at the outset, from parent to child, then reinforced by brothers, sisters, playmates, and finally the school. We have already seen how much of the language the child has acquired by the time he is six. This should lead us to realize that there is no such thing as linguistic original sin. Children do not commit solecisms out of native perversity. The departures from accepted usage which one encounters in their language are not their creation. They are features of the language transmitted by speakers of nonstandard dialects. And for every sub- or nonstandard feature at which the classroom teacher takes offense, the pupils have acquired scores of patterns and forms in which standard and nonstandard coincide. Let us take comfort in this, but at the same time recognize the strength of such constructions as the multiple negative, which is the product of oral transmission through a dozen generations since the time that it ceased to be written in the standard language, and three times as many before that. There is still every reason for trying to eliminate it, but we must recognize the amount of effort and drill that is necessary to replace a long-established linguistic habit with a new one.

I do not know that I have covered all the ingredients of what I would consider a healthy and helpful attitude toward language on the part of the teacher, but space forbids a more extended discussion of the matter. There are areas where a soundly based knowledge of the structure of the language can be put to work, particularly in connection with the expansion of language patterns. We must warn the student of the dangers involved in inadequately controlled expression and at the same time make him aware of resources and potentialities of the language about which he might otherwise remain innocent. In short, there is both a positive and a negative role for linguistic knowledge in the teaching of composition.

The negative role consists, in considerable part at least, in helping the student avoid structural ambiguities. It will be recalled that throughout his *Structure of English,* Fries points to syntactic situations where the grammatical meaning is vague and unclear because of the lack of unambiguous formal markers.[4] Following his lead, Norman C. Stageberg, in an article in the *English Journal,*[5] listed some twenty constructions or construction types which he considered responsible for most of the ambiguity in student writing. This is a move in the right direction, and without question more work in this field needs to be done.

Positively, most of us would like our students to achieve in their writing a greater degree of dexterity in the manipulation of the structural patterns of the language than is usual with them. In order to accomplish this, we must get them to recognize the patterns that they normally employ first of all, and then show them ways in which these may be expanded. Both the Lloyd and Warfel text, *American English in Its Cultural Setting,*[6] and Paul Roberts' various books[7] do this to a considerable extent, employing diagrams and formulas effectively to this end. Following some hints in Lloyd and Warfel, Sister Mary Aquin, writing in the February, 1960, issue of *College Composition and Communication,* demonstrates a step-by-step procedure for expanding one of the basic patterns.[8] She then goes on to apply the same pattern expansion technique to the paragraph and to the whole theme as well. Although tactics other than those suggested in her article may readily come to mind, I believe that her strategy is essentially correct, and that this is a positive way to get students to use the language more effectively. Even more recently, Francis Christensen has been urging what he calls a generative approach to rhetoric, which is also basically carefully controlled and built-up expansion.[9] But our success in all of this will depend upon an accurate and a skillful presentation of the basic language patterns.

This, however, raises the question, at what point in the student's education is this to be done? We have been unwise, I believe, in deferring a linguistically oriented approach to the language until either the freshman year in college, or at the earliest the concluding years of the secondary school. I am aware, of course, that some very good work has been done in the junior high school, particularly in Westport, Connecticut. Nevertheless, the longer we delay in this, the more we are forced to correct many of the notions and to revise the definitions that the student has already learned; in short, to alter radically his entire concept of language.

It is far preferable, I believe, to begin either at the end of the elementary school or at the beginning of the junior high school, and to focus first on the behavior of the spoken language, especially with respect to such suprasegmental features as intonation turns and accompanying terminal junctures; in short, to demonstrate how sentences work and what their basic patterns are. Lest there be no misunderstanding of my recommendation here, let me say flatly that I am not suggesting that we teach the terminology of structural linguistics or of generative grammar. I am recommending that we teach a recognition of language structure. Definitions should be formally based, but I include here position in the sentences and co-occurrences as well as liability to inflectional ending. The initial procedure should be largely inductive, but pattern drill should be employed, both as a means for assuring the recognition of and for expanding the basic pattterns.

All of this has the advantage of approaching the language problem in a way that is essentially positive, and this is so often what the teacher, functioning primarily in the role of proofreader, neglects or forgets. An incident involving one of my children a few years ago illustrates how sterile a negative approach to language can be. One of my daughters, at that time in the tenth grade, had written a review of Jacques Cousteau's *The Silent World*. One of the sentences in her theme read, "You can expect the unordinary under water." The teacher, understandably enough, marked this an error in diction, and when the writer attempted to defend her choice of the word, she was told that it was not in the particular dictionary required for class use. This merely presented a challenge to the child, who promptly went to the *Oxford English Dictionary,* discovered that the word had entered the language in 1547 and was, indeed, cited as late as 1909, which is about as late as one could expect the OED to cite anything. The discovery was promptly reported to the instructor, who then grudgingly accepted the word as legitimate.

By making this a question of whether or not the expression was permitted by authority, the teacher was in effect inviting the child to pit one authority against another with no possibility of a conclusive or satisfactory outcome. Had the student been invited to develop a synonymy of *unordinary,* showing where and how she felt that her use of the word differed in meaning and feeling from *out of the ordinary, extraordinary,* and *unusual,* her confidence in her earlier choice might have been somewhat shaken, and everyone, including the teacher, might have learned something.

Fundamentally, positiveness of attitude is what I have been stressing all along. It is what I feel we must develop, both within ourselves and in our students, in order to achieve the major goals with respect to the use of language that are educationally important. Positiveness does not mean permissiveness, but it does mean the development of a feeling that the language belongs to us, it is ours to use, that it is a medium, not a series of barriers, hedges, and fences. Or, if the barriers and hedges are there, they exist only to keep us on the track and not to check our progress.

Six

LINGUISTICS
AND THE TEACHING
OF SPELLING
AND READING

THE INTEREST OF LINGUISTS IN THE TEACHING OF READING WAS for a long time casual and peripatetic, and has only recently taken on the qualities of serious commitment and permanence. Leonard Bloomfield's original article, "Linguistics and Reading," which appeared in 1942 in the *Elementary English Review*,[1] just about the same time that the parochial schools of Chicago were experimenting with materials which he had developed, was followed by a long silence. In fact, it could be said that Bloomfield's concern with this topic was in a sense anticipated by his statement in 1925, when he wrote in his justification for the formation of a Linguistic Society, "Our schools are conducted by persons who, from professors of education down to teachers in the classroom, know nothing of the results of linguistic science, not even the relation of writing to speech or of standard language to dialect. In short, they do not know what language is, and in consequence, waste years of every child's life and reach a poor result."[2]

Although this early interest in reading seemed to have been forgotten during the hectic war years and in the early 1950's, Charles C. Fries has a tenacious memory about such matters, and the problem never really disappeared from his line of vision. He discussed it on a number of occasions and tried out some small-scale experiments, but it was not until some time after his retirement from the University of Michigan in 1958 that he began to devote a major share of his attention to the teaching of reading. He then became deeply involved with this problem in the public schools of Philadelphia. Henry Lee Smith, Jr. had also become engaged in the linguistic orientation of elementary school teachers and the preparation of reading materials during the mid 1950's, working with the teaching staff in one of the counties of Maryland. Since that time a number of others, including Raven I. McDavid, Jr., Pauline Rojas, and Priscilla Tyler have become interested and active.

It is true that over the years many linguists have been concerned with problems of literacy, but far more often this has been confined to speakers of hitherto unwritten languages. Here the contribution of the linguist has consisted in the main of the development of what seemed a consistent alphabet and a rational writing system. As regards the teaching of reading in this country, to native speakers of English in particular, it again seems to be a field where the linguist conceivably has something to contribute but also one in which his contribution will be most useful in collaboration with persons from other disciplines.

The teaching of reading and of spelling are also fields in which the historian of the English language can supply some background information which, though not in itself immediately applicable, will provide a frame of reference and an enlightening context for certain aspects of the problem. Clearly the best place to begin is by discussing the overall efficiency of the English writing system, for after all that is what we must cope with as we attempt to teach children to read. It is well known that the difficulties inherent in it are possibly the greatest barrier to an even wider spread of English as an international auxiliary language than it enjoys today. Actually, over the past five years the linguists have been somewhat less critical of the writing system than they used to be and have even begun to point out certain hitherto unperceived virtues. Nevertheless, it clearly suffers in comparison with such languages as Spanish and German.

The difficulties and inconsistencies in our mode of spelling and writing arise from four or five sets of circumstances. Looming large among these is the fact that English has a far greater number of significantly different sounds than there are vowel letters or characters to indicate them. Most phonological analyses of English recognize as many as thirteen, sometimes even fifteen, different vowel sounds. In the Trager-Smith treatment, there are nine distinctive short vowels alone.[3] These differences aside, the fact remains that five vowel letters cannot adequately serve this extensive repertoire, and as a consequence, combinations of vowel letters have been employed with what almost amounts to abandon. The fact that *ee, ei, ie, ea, eo, ey, ay* have all been pressed into service (as in *deem, receive, believe, mean, people, key, quay*) to indicate a single sound is an indication of the confusion that has come to prevail.

Moreover, of these more than a dozen vowel sounds, a number are roughly paired into what in ordinary talk about language we speak of as "long" and "short." Actually the relationship between them is not a quantitative one, but however that may be, we have come to employ three different graphic devices to indicate it. There are times when a single vowel character indicates what is thought of as a short vowel, whereas a double vowel spelling signals the corresponding long, as in *bet* and *beet*. On other occasions, an unpronounced final *-e* will indicate the distinction between the two, as in *mat* and *mate*. Still another device is the doubling of the consonant letter following the vowel, not, to be sure, to show us anything about the quality or quantity of the consonant sound, but again to convey some information about the vowel which precedes it, as in *ridden, bitten, bottom,* and *better.* Add to these the practice of employing *i* and *a* in such combinations as *maid* and *coat,* and we end up with such strange series as *mad, madder, made,* and *maid; cot, cotton, coat,* and *cote,* to say nothing of *weigh* and *dough.*

There is also the historical accident of the great vowel shift, which took place some time between 1400 and 1600. This produced a series of changes in the pronunciation of the so-called long vowels which profoundly affected the relationship between vowel sound and vowel symbol or character. It is only in English that the first letter of the alphabet is pronounced with or called by the vowel sound of the word *mate*; every other western European language associates it with the stressed sound of *father.* Similarly, the fifth letter of the alphabet, elsewhere associated with the vowel of *mate*, has for us the quality of the vowel in *deem.* The shift in value has applied with equal force to the letters *i* and *u*. Probably the most important consequence of this is that the relationship between short and long pairs, which originally had a natural phonetic affinity, has been disturbed. It is the sounds of *bit* and *beat* which are phonetically similar, not *bit* and *bite.*

There were cetrain other developments, involving consonants as well as vowels, which were never reflected in the spelling. The sound, comparable to that in German *nacht* or *licht,* which in English ultimately came to be spelled *gh* in words like *might, laugh,* or *dough,* either disappeared or developed into some other consonant approximately in the fourth quarter of the fifteenth century. Now, almost 400 years later, we still continue to spell it in the majority of words that once had it. Other changes in sound, such as the initial consonant of *sure* and *sugar* (originally [s]), the medial sound of *vision* (originally [z] and now the same as French *rouge*), the *sh* in *-tion* are likewise without a visible reflection in the way we continue to write the words. Our present system of indicating the initial consonants of *thin* and *then* is less satisfactory than the one that King Alfred used.

The great influx of Latin and French words into English has added to our difficulties in another way. The native English word stock still adheres to the Germanic pattern of fixed stress upon the root syllable, no matter how many derivative affixes may be added to the base: witness *kind, kindly, unkind, kindness, kindest, kindliest.* On the other hand, borrowed series such as *family, familiar, familiarity* or *aristocrat, aristocracy, aristocratic* reflect the shifting stress patterns of the languages from which they were derived as well as the gradation or neutralization of the unstressed vowels. Our spelling offers no clues to either of these phenomena.

These, among others, are the factors which make for difficulty in the spelling of English, which in turn makes of the teaching of reading a longer and more continuous process in English-speaking countries than elsewhere. It must readily be conceded that knowing some or all of the factors that cause the difficulty by no means effects a cure, but actually there is a limited realm of application of even this much, confessedly somewhat diluted, historical knowledge.

For one thing, it provides a rationale for some of the changes in spelling which occur when inflections and suffixes are added: *hope, hoping; hop, hopping.* An understanding of the dual function of *y* (vowel in final and preconsonantal position, consonant in prevocalic position) explains *lady, ladies* and *happy, happiest*. Moreover, it helps to account for, though not at all completely, some of our practices in word division. Certain old-fashioned and seldom used spellings can be understood as reflections of earlier but no longer current pronunciations: *shew* and *plough*. A little historical information also throws light upon the use of distinctive spellings to differentiate such homophonic pairs as *sew* and *sow, sun* and *son*, and also on the development of such homographs as the present and past tense forms of *read*, and the noun and verb pair spelled *lead*.

As with some of the questions discussed in the preceding chapter, attitude toward language is of major importance. If the teacher is led to see that our orthography, chaotic as it appears at first glance, does after all reflect not one, but two, three, or four systems none of which is applied or carried out to its ultimate conclusion, and that there are historical explanations for some of the inconsistencies and anachronisms that we find, this again helps to build up the feeling that the language and its writing system are not something indescribable, inscrutable, unexplainable, and uncontrollable, but that in their own highly peculiar way, they do make some sense.

None of this will teach you to spell or to recognize a single word, nor it is information that will be of practical value to your pupils. Indeed, I should not recommend passing it on to them except as incidental information when a question is raised, if at all. But it does constitute an extra resource of knowledge about the language, so important in developing a sense of command and confidence.

It should be said that over the past five or ten years the attitude of linguists toward the spelling system has undergone at least a degree of change. A dozen years ago, virtually all of them would have had nothing but criticism to offer. As long as they looked at it only in terms of phonemic-graphemic correspondence, that is to say, the relationship of sound and letter, it did seem full of inconsistencies, though even here the irregularities always loomed larger than the regularities.

Since then, particularly in the past six or seven years, the morphophoneme has come to take on a hitherto unrealized importance. Viewed in the light of this, certain practices assume new aspects of economy and even regularity. It is true enough, for example, that viewed strictly in terms of phonetics, the regular plural inflection of English nouns has three forms rather than one: [s] after voiceless consonants except the three voiceless sibilants, [z] after voiced sound except the three voiced sibilants, and [əz] after the final sounds of *hiss, rose, dish, rouge, church,* and *edge.* However, since this alternation is wholly automatic with native speakers of the language, no one ever having to give it a thought and the majority of speakers totally unaware that these differences even exist, there is really no need for the spelling to do more than to signal plurality. (This does not apply, of course, to materials designed to teach English as a foreign language.) Shifts in the pronunciation of the genitive singular inflections and those for the past tense and past participle of regular verbs are likewise part of the unconscious and automatically controlled grammatical mechanism of every native speaker of English. Each of these can be taken care of adequately by a single spelling symbol.

Likewise, for a number of reasons which need not be treated in detail here, base forms in English sometimes alter the pronunciation of their final consonant in more than one way when derivative suffixes are added: for example, *logic, logicity, logician; electric, electricity, electrician.* If a phonetic spelling shifted from *k* to *s* to *sh* in words like these, the gain in accuracy would probably be offset by the lack of any visible relationship among the members of the series. Thus, even within the apparent chaos. everything is not all bad.

This last circumstance may be one reason why the Initial Teaching Alphabet, based upon what purports to be a phonemic representation of English, could be somewhat less appealing to-day than it might have been fifteen years ago. There would be little point in getting into a discussion of its merits and demerits here; it is new enough so that reactions to it often tend to be emotional rather than rational. There is no escaping the fact, how-ever, that the linguistic premise upon which it is based no longer seems quite as important to, nor is as firmly held by, the linguists as it once was. Nevertheless, it is important to recognize that the ITA is intended to be just what its name specifies, an initial alpha-bet serving as a first step in teaching children to read.

All teachers of English are asked about simplified spelling from time to time. Will it come about? If not, why not? It seems so sensible. A bill providing for its establishment has been offered every year in Congress for the past several sessions. Nothing is impossible, of course, but if the past offers any index to the future, any revolutionary change in our spelling and writing system is difficult to conceive. Our history is dotted with energetic and well-intentioned spelling reformers. As far back as the thirteenth cen-tury, Orm, an English monk, wrote a long and intolerably dull poem according to a spelling practice of his own devising. It is to him that we owe the practice of doubling the following conso-nant to indicate a short vowel, and we have followed it in part. Even before Orm, Anglo-Saxon scribes on occasion used to double a vowel character to indicate length; we have followed this also, in part, in that we employ the practice with the letters *e* and *o* but not *a, i,* or *u.* To some now unknown fifteenth-century man with an idea we owe the practice of adding *a* to the letters *o* and *e* to indicate vowel length, and again we have followed it, in part. The roll of those who from that time on tried to help matters along includes men of all descriptions and occupations from schoolmasters to scientists, from John Hart to Bishop Wilkins—the latter was a fellow and a founder of the Royal Society. All told, their efforts had almost a negligible effect.

Noah Webster, filled with enthusiasm for developing a national language at the time that he edited his *American Dictionary of the English Language*, rode roughshod over some of our most cherished and wasteful spelling practices. He amputated final -*e*'s with impunity, threw out such wasteful consonant digraphs as *gh*, substituted *f* for *ph*, operating in what was generally a reasonable and logical manner. Again, he succeeded only in small part; we have retained possibly 15 per cent of what he tried to establish, notably the simplification of -*our* to -*or* in words like *favour* and *colour*, and the reversal of the two final letters in such words as *centre* and *theatre*. Fowler's comment on the English reaction to -*or* spellings is a good indication of the typical Anglo-Saxon reaction to spelling reform.

The American abolition of -*our* in such words as *honour* and *favour* has probably retarded rather than quickened English progress in the same direction. Our first notification that the book we are reading is not English but American is often, nowadays, the sight of an -*or*. 'Yankee' we say, & congratulate ourselves on spelling like gentlemen; we wisely decline to regard it as a matter for argument; the English way cannot but be better than the American way; that is enough. . . . Those who are willing to put national prejudice aside & examine the facts quickly realize, first, that the British -*our* words are much fewer in proportion to the -*or* words than they supposed, &, secondly, that there seems to be no discoverable line between the two sets so based on principle as to serve any useful purpose. By the side of *favour* there is *horror*, beside *ardour pallor*, beside *odour tremor,* & so forth. . . . What is likely to happen is that either, when some general reform of spelling is consented to, reduction of *-our* to *-or* will be one of the least disputed items, or, failing general reform, we shall see word after word in *-our* go the way of *governour.* It is not worth while either to resist such a gradual change or to fly in the face of national sentiment by trying to hurry it; it would need a very open mind indeed in an Englishman to accept *armor* and *succor* with equanimity.[4]

Americans would undoubtedly react in much the same way if the circumstances were reversed. There is, if anything, a greater veneration of spelling on this side of the Atlantic.

It may be worth observing, moreover, that sweeping changes in writing systems have often taken place in consequence of a social or political upheaval. Turkey substituted the Latin for the Arabic alphabet in the early years of the government of Kemal Pasha Ataturk. Russia instituted certain reforms in the Cyrillic alphabet also in the 1920's, not too long after the revolution. In general, social and political stability seem to favor the continuance of existing writing systems. Therefore, barring a social upheaval or an automated change so great that we cannot now conceive of its nature, we shall undoubtedly continue to go on our way of cautious compromise.

Many of the linguistic considerations that have been mentioned are beginning to have some effect on the teaching of spelling. Originally we concentrated on long and difficult words, often those with little or no practical potential use. We have given this up in the schools and retain the practice chiefly in connection with national spelling contests, conducted with an eye to the public relations of certain commercial enterprises rather than in the interest of sound educational practice. A newspaper article which appeared just as these lines were being written asserted that, "words like *piccalilli, terrapin, syllepsis* and *cinnabar* have suddenly become more important for more than 500,000 school children. . . ." The number refers to the children in just the New York metropolitan area. The words, of course, have not become important. Their spellings have done so, on the grounds of no conceivable utility except that of winning a contest.

Emphasis upon the jawbreaking or particularly confusing words gave way to stress upon useful ones, as determined by frequency counts. After a period of concentration upon them, attention again shifted to those items in the vocabulary which showed the most regular phonemic-graphemic relationships. We are now tending to present the most regular patterns first, moving gradually to the more complex and irregular.

In the teaching of reading, just as with spelling, the contribution of linguistics thus far has been much more in the way of providing the teacher with a context for what he does than in any specific materials which have been developed up to this time. Some three or four ideas in particular have come to be recognized as important for the reading teacher and have been gaining currency. Some of them constitute refreshing correctives to earlier pedagogical lore.

Of these, probably the most important is the recognition that teaching a child to read is not teaching him "language" or "the language." We have already pointed out that the child, when he enters school, has a better than fair mastery of the entire phonological system and a vocabulary of some thousands of words. Consequently, "Run, Dick, run!" is scarcely calculated to lead him into any new *linguistic* experience. It merely serves to teach him how to interpret and employ the writing system of a language which he already controls with a degree of competence.

Assuming that the child does not know how to read when he enters school, and assuming that he learns to read at approximately the rate that the average course of study provides, it will be about three years before his mastery of the graphic system catches up and is on a par with his mastery of the language, which is also developing at its own rate. Only then will he be able to use reading as a means of enlarging, extending, and enriching his linguistic experience.

Most of the current generation of children have had some contact with the writing system before entering school. Even if they come from homes where the parents never pick up a book and rarely a newspaper, they have seen commercial advertising on television, if nothing else. Even here letters and sounds are associated, and indeed, animated letters and words behave at times in astonishing and intriguing ways. It is scarcely realistic, therefore, to presume on the part of the child a total innocence of the connection between language and the cabalistic configurations on paper or the glass screen.

Finally, we are very certain that the child's mastery of the language at the age-range from six to nine is far more complex than the language of most children's readers intended for use in the first three grades of elementary school. The studies of Ruth Strickland[5] and Walter Loban[6] have demonstrated this in a most convincing fashion.

In general, such elementary reading materials as the linguists have developed depend basically upon the most frequent and regular phonemic-graphemic correspondence patterns (which is, in a sense, another way of saying the most regular spellings) and upon the principle of minimal or contrastive pairs as devices to fix in the child's mind the connection between the sound and its graphic representation. In fact, they even depend upon minimal contrasts to teach the child to identify the shapes of letters— E as contrasted with F, P with B, and so on.

Linguistically oriented materials do not regard or present letters as having sounds, but instead they present the sound as having a typical representation. This is an important difference between a linguistic and a phonic approach, one which is often not fully comprehended. Rudolf Flesch in his highly catalytic volume *Why Johnny Can't Read* completely failed to grasp this distinction.

By now, linguists have been responsible for possibly a half-dozen reading programs. They differ in detail, but they usually begin with the most regular ways of indicating the short vowel sounds, employing, as I have indicated, series of words with minimal contrasts, such as *Let Bet get a pet* or *Nan can fan Dan*. They then make use of various strategies to encompass the rest of the graphic system, often proceeding to spellings of the *rain* or *pane* type. These approaches appear to have had some success in establishing the connection between sound and symbol, thus giving the child a technique for attacking words that he has not previously encountered. How successful they are or will be beyond this point is somewhat less clear. There seem to be some grounds for suspecting that although sound and symbol are quite successfully connected in the mind of the child, he comes out of it all with not much zest for reading. But it may well be that this is due in part to the newness of the technique and to lack of experience in devising materials that have a story interest or some other kind of appeal.

Up to the present, however, most of the linguists seem to have given surprisingly little attention to larger units of language, phrase and sentence structure in particular. Carl Lefevre, who has also been interested in the application of linguistics to the teaching of reading, does seem to have realized that there ought to be some connection between whole structures, syntactical patterns, and the process of reading comprehension. In his review of the Bloomfield and Barnhart *Let's Read,* he has made his point very cogently:

> Reading is basically a language-related process that must be studied rigorously in relation to what is known about the structure of the American language . . . *in relation to all that is known today,* not merely spelling related to segmental phonemes. *Reading instruction must take into account intonation patterns, patterns of syntax* (including expansions, substitutions, transformations), *structure words and word-form changes.* It seems probable that these four signaling systems are much more important to reading instruction than spelling is. . . . The fundamental problem of reading instruction is to teach the relationship of the graphic system, writing and print, to the language as a whole—that is, to speech.[7]

Two other aspects of the linguists' approach to reading merit at least brief mention. In general their materials concede, by implication if not overtly, that certain words will have to be taught as wholes, just as numbers are, without reference to sound-symbol correspondence. They do recognize an ideographic element here. Moreover, in the linguistically oriented materials, frequency is not an overriding factor which is permitted to control the choice of vocabulary items. After all, if the vocabulary of the six-year old is to be reckoned in the thousands, the matter of limiting the pre-primer to the first one or two hundred most frequently used words becomes of little significance. On the other hand, a considerable amount of attention is given to reintroducing the same words at regular intervals until their recognition becomes automatic.

To conclude, it is fair to say that the linguists have added some new dimensions to the teaching of reading, which will undoubtedly influence a fair number of beginning reading textbooks in one way or another. They have not provided the entire answer to the reading problem by any means, nor are they likely to. The time is ripe, however, for cooperation among linguists, reading specialists, learning theorists, child psychologists, and successful writers of children's stories. Together they can develop materials which will demonstrate to the child that reading is fun, that it can be mastered, and that it is rewarding and useful.

Seven

LINGUISTICS
AND THE STUDY
OF LITERATURE

As we proceed from reading to the use of the written language as a literary medium we enter upon another area where the linguist has a potential contribution to make. Actually, it is strange that this has to be called to anyone's attention. Fifty years ago a discussion which was intended to establish some common bases of understanding between students of language and historians or critics of literature would have been a work of supererogation, to say the least.

At that time linguistic scholars were for the most part teachers of literature as well, and what then passed for linguistic, or, more properly, philological study was a regular part of the training of everyone whose major interest was in literature. Moreover, it was not at all unusual for such men as Kittredge, Manly, and Brandl to produce perceptive literary essays and critical evaluations as well as major contributions to our knowledge of the history and the structure of the English language.

Since their time the increasing tendency toward specialization and the realignment of these special branches of learning has resulted in a wide and unfortunate separation of literary and linguistic studies. On the one hand, the linguistic preparation of majors in literature has almost reached the vanishing point in most American colleges and universities. At the same time, the unprecedented development of linguistics during the second quarter of the twentieth century involved, as we have already seen, a totally different approach to language phenomena, a whole new range of concepts, and a new terminology. Consequently, anyone who received his linguistic training before 1935 needs almost a complete re-education in order to understand what the present-day linguistic scholars are talking about. During this period linguistics has tended to move out of the orbit of the humanities toward that of the social sciences.

Nor has literary scholarship been without its changes of direction and emphasis, among which must be included the development, some years ago, of the so-called "new" criticism. It is scarcely to the point here to debate the merits of this particular critical approach, but it is worth noting that the newness of this criticism was presumed to consist in part of disregarding the heavy emphasis upon historical considerations which supposedly characterized the more traditional literary scholarship and of emphasizing the close analysis of the work of art itself. In short, when the critic is dealing with a literary work, this implies "the closest possible examination of what the poem says as a poem," to quote Cleanth Brooks. Asking what the poem says is in essence a linguistic question. To this extent, critic and linguist are in fundamental agreement, for the latter is also likely to insist that any literary work, be it sonnet or novel, is essentially a linguistic act, differing from other stretches of language in that it displays a higher degree of selectivity.

It is this circumstance which leads to the first question to be posed. On the one hand we have had, during the past thirty years, a scientific or systematic approach to language, one which has made rapid progress not only in the United States but in many parts of Europe as well, resulting in a considerable modification of traditional attitudes about the structure and operation of language. On the other hand, an important group of literary scholars has demonstrated an intense concern for language, particularly as it has been employed by the great authors who used English as the vehicle for their literary masterpieces. What, then, are the ideas about language which are to be found in the writings of some of the contemporary critics? What concepts of linguistic structure do they employ, since they do concern themselves particularly with the structural analysis of literary works? What assumptions about language are implicit in their writing? Or, to put the matter in another light, to what extent will the contemporary linguistic scientist find himself in agreement with the ideas about language which he is likely to find in the writings of the "new" critics or indeed the newer ones who have succeeded them?

These questions are raised not with the intent of making invidious comparisons or drawing devastating conclusions, but rather to explore the possibilities of what now must be called an interdisciplinary approach. Surely the linguist and the critic have much to learn from each other, and the teacher can profit from the points of view of both. It would be to the benefit of humanistic studies as a whole if the views of linguist and critic toward literature might be synthesized, as they so often were at the beginning of the century, in the person of a single scholar.

Among the attitudes toward language reflected in much critical writing even today is one which might be characterized as linguistic primitivism. A typical expression of this runs as follows:

> There are two outstanding respects in which primitive language, and especially spoken language, tends to be poetic, or at any rate to have a natural kinship with poetry: first in its manner of utterance, its rhythms and euphonies; second, in its manner of reference, in the delicacy and associative fullness with which it refers to various aspects of the all-encompassing Mystery. In short, primitive speech—for I am dealing here with language that is meant to be spoken—employs both rhythm and metaphor. Primitive speech is a more direct expression of the community than speech by which the sense of community is projected and carried through time.[1]

Although Wheelwright, the author of this statement, is on what might be considered sound linguistic grounds in his assumption or acceptance of the primacy of the spoken language, his statement exhibits a rather widespread ethnocentric misconception, namely, that the languages of peoples outside the western European cultural orbit are necessarily to be considered on the same basis as the earliest historical (or prehistorical) stages of the Indo-European languages. It is interesting to observe that although he follows the statement quoted above with an illustration drawn from the Fiji Islands, he precedes it with a quotation from Shelley to the effect that "in the infancy of society every author is a poet because language itself is poetry." John Crowe Ransome too assumes, "First a Golden Age, such as Ovid describes; or a Garden of Eden period . . . a period in which there was only one language. Call it the age of neither prose nor poetry, or the age when prose and poetry were one."[2]

Obviously the sober realities of linguistic evidence force the scientist to characterize this somewhat naive primitivism as unprovable. If we are speaking of primitive language in the historical sense, we must remember that systems of writing take us back no more than five or six thousand years at the most. Fifty thousand years is now considered a most conservative estimate of the length of time that the human race has been speaking; figures in excess of 100,000 years are not at all unusual. Consequently the written records cannot be held to contain evidence of language in anything like its earliest stages, nor can anything be adduced as to its prosodic or rhythmical character or as to the metaphorical qualities of its vocabulary. If, on the other hand, we mean by primitive languages non-Indo-European languages which have not been reduced to writing and thus representing non-literate cultures, it would indeed be difficult to conceive of any set of assumptions which would be equally valid for Kazakh, Fanti, and Tarascan.

A somewhat related idea is that of the poet as the maker or creator of language, suggested part of the time at least by etymological considerations. Cleanth Brooks tells us, for example, that the poet is remaking language, that he has to make up his language as he goes, and that he is most truthfully described as a *poites* or maker. Similar sentiments may be found in any number of recent critical writings, and not infrequently these go so far as to insist that Dante, or Chaucer, or some other major literary figure "created a language in itself music and persuasion out of a chaos of inharmonious barbarisms." The phrase happens to be Shelley's, but the idea lives on. Now, let us ask in all seriousness what we are to understand by *creating* or *remaking* a language? Does it mean establishing a standard form? Historical research clearly indicates that in the western European countries generally, the factors which operated to lend prestige to a particular dialect were political, economic, and social in character. Only after a dialect had acquired such prestige were men of letters likely to employ it. Chaucer, it is true, wrote in London English, which was his native dialect, but so did Gower, born in Kent, and Wycliffe, who came from the north of England.

If remaking a language does not necessarily imply the establishment of a standard form, does it mean adding words to the lexicon? This is difficult to prove, for the historical dictionary, often quite stringently limited as to the extent of the evidence it may present, is more likely to cite the poet than his more prosaic contemporaries. Moreover, in this connection we must also consider the attitude of such a linguist as Robert A. Hall, Jr., who will insist that even such palpable individual coinages as van Helmont's *gas* and George Eastman's *kodak* are scarcely to be considered as creation since they are formed in keeping with the phonemic patterns already prevailing in the language.

Does remaking the language consist of adding new meanings to words already in the vocabulary? This is somewhat more plausible, since it may be maintained that ideally considered, no two contextual situations are ever absolutely identical, and consequently, every particular use of a word differs somewhat in meaning from every other use, but again, on a practical basis, evidence for this is as unsatisfactory as it is for word coinages.

Finally, there would be the question of whether the poet remakes language by establishing new inflectional or syntactic forms. This can virtually be dismissed out of hand, for there is no evidence to support it in any language that I know of. If it were true, it would to the linguist constitute creation on the most significant plane, for the morphological and syntactic structures of a language are even more fundamental to the manner in which a speech community classifies or categorizes experience than is its lexicon.

The linguist and his literary colleagues find themselves even farther apart when the latter try to deal with the way in which some particular author manipulated the English language. Here the preoccupation of the literary historian with a single outstanding literary figure tends to obscure the general development of the language along the lines of general social utility. In fact, the critic is so likely to be convinced of the stature of his author in contributing to the language that he often neglects to consult the ordinary sources of information. Shakespeare, in particular, is constantly given credit for inventions which are not his. In speaking of his use of *to famous* as a verb, Ransome remarks, "Shakespeare makes a verb of an adjective, but his coinage could not give it currency, for it is not that kind of adjective."[3]

Disregarding for the moment the specious reasoning of the second clause, let us simply consult the record. The *Oxford English Dictionary* clearly demonstrates that this change of function was not original with Shakespeare. A citation from Lodge antedates his use of it in the Sonnets, as does another from Tarleton. There is a still earlier one from Stanyhurst with a slight variation in the spelling. As for the term not attaining currency, there are eight citations well distributed throughout the seventeenth century, and the word is found as late as the third quarter of the nineteenth, both in dialect and in Standard English. Similarly, B. Ifor Evans credits Shakespeare's use of *to camp* and *to unhair* as verbs as skillful inventions indicating the "alertness of his mind with vocabulary." Again, we find the first of these used verbally as early as 1543 and the second in Wycliffe.

Examples could be multiplied *ad infinitum,* but it is not at all the purpose here to upbraid anyone for his failure to use the most obvious source work on the history of the English vocabulary. Much more disturbing is the extent to which it is assumed that any one individual is likely to alter and influence the language. Because some of the words cited in the foregoing paragraphs were recorded before Shakespeare does not necessarily mean that Shakespeare saw them in these sources, or elsewhere for that matter. He may, or he may not have. He may have heard them spoken, or his own use of them may have been invention as far as he was concerned. But the fact remains that the functional change of noun or adjective to verb was a common phenomenon at this period, just as it is today. Possibly hundreds of such changes were creations of the moment, in ordinary conversation, by ordinary people, and were never written down. Others, essentially no less striking or unusual, did get set down in writing. But to claim this process as the prerogative of one man, when it clearly was widely spread throughout the vocabulary and among all speakers of the language, seems somewhat reckless and uncritical, to say the least.

The relationship between sound and meaning is a topic which also invites a certain amount of rashness, an inevitable consequence of the disregard of historical and comparative data on the one hand, and phonemic and structural concepts on the other. Attitudes vary considerably on this point, ranging from the skepticism of Ransome, demonstrated in his well-known parody of Tennyson's line, "the murdering of innumerable beeves," to the insistence by Carl R. Woodring upon the validity of sound symbolism.[4] Warren and Wellek, in their *Theory of Literature,* take a sound middle-of-the-road point of view on this matter; consequently it is scarcely necessary to go into detail about it here. A few considerations, chiefly historical, deserve mention, however. Since sounds and classes of sounds do change in the course of time within a language, an onomatopoetic or symbolic effect that is operative for one century need not necessarily be valid in another. Where *bow-wow* (pronounced *boo-woo*) was a reasonably successful imitation of a dog's bark before the great vowel shift, today it is scarcely more than a conventional symbol. Similarly, the phonemic realignments of sounds and sound combinations cannot safely be ignored. For example, throughout all of the Old English period and in fact up to 1200, *f* and *v* were not distinct phonemes as they are today, but were simply variant members of a single class of sound, their use depending wholly upon their position in the word with respect to adjacent sounds. Consequently, for this period it would be difficult to interpret the voiceless allophone *f* as "panting" and the voiced variant *v* as suggesting langorous rapture, as they have been characterized within the past decade.

It must be recognized, too, that the symbolic or suggestive value of sounds will vary from one language to another. Woodring, in polling a group of students on their reactions to *Jabberwocky,* concludes that the long *i* and long *a* sounds suggest "brightness, lightness, ease, and gaiety."[5] Yet, for a native speaker of Spanish, for whom the interjection *ay* (pronounced much as long *i* in Modern English) is equivalent to English *Alas!* or *Woe is me!* this sound might well have decidedly unpleasant connections.

It is possible that for English a careful study of consonant clusters would be more rewarding in this connection than anything that has hitherto been undertaken, but it is doubtful that any extended examination of the entire question would lead to conclusions that might be applied to more than a few narrowly limited segments of the vocabulary. The important thing is to get rid of dubious statements about panting *f*'s languid *l*'s, dark and light vowels, and the like. Comparisons of sound with color, lung capacity, and tactile sensations will not take us far along the path to a sensible and defensible aesthetic of sound.

Naturally the student of literature is deeply concerned with the problem of meaning, and here his interests are linked more closely with semantics than with structural linguistics. On the whole, the study of meaning has only recently begun to develop something of the same rigorous methodology which characterizes the present-day analysis of other features of language. Consequently, we should not be too greatly surprised at finding looseness of concept and of terminology here, for probably little else could reasonably be expected.

Discussions of meaning often begin with a differentiation between the vocabularies of science and of poetry in terms something like the following:

> [The scientist] demands an exact one-to-one relevance of language to the objects and events to which it refers.
> The tendency of science is necessarily to stabilize terms, to forge them into strict denotations; the poet's tendency is by contrast disruptive. The terms are thus continually modifying each other, and thus violating their dictionary meanings.[6]

This assumed dichotomy between the vocabulary of science and that of poetry usually serves, then, as the springboard for a discussion of denotation and connotation, which next leads to a consideration of metaphor, and we ultimately arrive at the figurative use of language characteristic of the metaphysical poets, so highly valued by many of the recent critics. Let us return for the moment, however, to the supposed differences between scientific and poetic language.

It may be reasonably maintained that the language of science is by no means as exact or as incapable of multiple interpretation as some of our literary colleagues would have us believe. The exact one-to-one relationship between words and their referents can and does occur chiefly with respect to natural objects. Even here this is true chiefly of botanical and zoological names indicating genus and species, or with such catalogs as those of the chemical elements. But it might well be argued that *sodium chloride* or *lycopersicon esculentum* are code rather than language.

At all events, these familiar statements about the language of science apply chiefly to its taxonomic aspects. When it comes to consideration of process, operation, and causation, the scientific vocabularies are a long way from being standardized or stabilized. Furthermore, this appears to be quite as true of the applied as of the so-called pure sciences. I have been told by a metallurgical engineer that there is far from common agreement upon the basic terminology in that field. A physicist has said that the vocabulary of the theoretical phases of that science serves chiefly to bring about some common orientation to matters under discussion, but it does not go much beyond that. At any rate, this is sufficient to demonstrate that the supposed exactness of the scientific vocabulary is in itself an inaccurate generalization which all of us would do well to discard if we are disposed to consider language as it does exist rather than in terms of what we assume to be the case.

A related distinction which is often encountered in the critical analysis of literature is that between *denotation,* the purely referential meaning of a term, and *connotation,* the affective and associative aura of meanings which cluster around a word. No doubt the distinction is useful in the abstract, but questions do arise when it is applied specifically. In particular, how does one determine where denotation leaves off and connotation begins?

My own experience with a particular phrase will serve to illustrate what is meant by the question. I first encountered the expression *Ancient of Days* as the title of one of William Blake's engravings, and it was only afterward that I became aware of the biblical context which served as the suggestion for the drawing. Before this, however, I had also been familiar with the seventeenth-century use of the substantive *ancient* to mean "ensign," as Shakespeare uses it in *Othello* for example. This knowledge, combined with the imagery in Emerson's poem *Days* ("Damsels of Time . . . marching single in an endless file"), was sufficient to suggest the concept of the Almighty as a commander of an endless procession of units of time. The figure and design are attractive, to a degree at least, but in reality there is no basis in fact for this interpretation of *ancient* in the phrase in question. It is purely and simply a substantive use of the adjective. My point is, however, that a particular succession of linguistic experiences, peculiar to a single individual and not likely to be duplicated, gave rise to certain associative experiences and hence connotive values which no author could possibly have intended or anticipated. If this is the case, how confident can the critic be that the specific connotations which he recognizes in or projects from a given context are valid for any significant body of his readers?

Diachronic changes of meaning pose an additional series of questions. If over the past five or six centuries the denotation of a word has altered materially, can we with any accuracy hope to recapture the connotations which it had at an earlier period? Could any American, for example, read Cowper's line, "self-imprisoned in their proud saloons," without some associative interference from the past and present American English use of the word? Will not the current sense of *starve* cause the modern reader to react to the seventeenth-century line, "Poore Venus, starv's with cold and soon will die," in a way which its author could neither have intended nor foreseen? All of this suggests that in order to eliminate confusion in matters of this kind, further clarification of definition and rigor in methodology are urgently needed.

This need seems particularly acute in the light of current references to Bateson's theory of semantic development, which proceeds upon the premise that a language, considered semantically, evolves through a series of conflicts between the denotative and the connotative forces in words; between an asceticism tending to kill language by stripping words of all association, and a hedonism tending to kill language by dissipating their sense in a multiplicity of associations.[7] In the light of this, the early and mid-seventeenth century is viewed as a connotative period. Then the scientific influence brought about a denotative period which extended through the eighteenth century, producing such plain, unimaginative language that a special poetic diction had to be created. To this there was a Romantic reaction, in which connotation came into its own again, and so on.

This is a plausible and engaging theory, despite the questionable assertion about languages being killed from a famine or a surfeit of associative meaning. I know of none that ever was. However, it remains little more than a hypothesis based upon writings about language. Whether or not it is capable of empirical proof, I am not certain, but assuredly no one has attempted to test it by means of a controlled sampling of the vocabulary or by a systematic investigation into specific areas of the lexicon.

One faces much the same problem with figurative uses of language. Perhaps no single term has occasioned quite as much glib self-assurance recently as the word *metaphor,* yet I must confess to a considerable degree of doubt as to what constitutes one. For example, I consult the *Oxford English Dictionary* under the entry *map.* The first definition is what is normally understood by the literal meaning of the term. Next, I encounter what are classified as transferred meanings, some applied to tables or charts, but another to a purely mental arrangement or concept. Is the last of these metaphorical, or is it not? Evidently it was not so considered by the editor, for he did not label it figurative.

Next, I find two more meanings—a tract of country spread out like a map, and a figure resembling a map in form or outline. These are still classified as transferred. Then we come to what the editor does label as figurative, and certainly Rowland's expression *map of sorrow* does seem metaphorical in its context, but Burke's "the map of their situation," in the same division of the word treatment, appears to be less so. Likewise, among the citations for *map* as a verb, the supposedly transferred and figurative use from Shakespeare's *Cymbeline*—"I am neere to the place where they should meet, if Pisiano have mapped it truly"— seems quite literal compared with Rider Haggard's "The form of a man vaguely mapped upon the twilight." It is quite possible that these personal classifications may not be acceptable to anyone else, but this does not invalidate the point that there is little general agreement as to where literal transference or extension leaves off and figurative usage begins. True enough, an attempt has been made to differentiate between faded metaphor—*leg of a table, foot of a mountain*—and the poetic figure, but again the same problem crops up. How about the leg of a triangle, of a race-course, to make a leg, to keep one's legs, or Dryden's line, "Their trusty staff (their better leg) supplied," in which *leg* and *staff* are in apposition?

What does I. A. Richards literally mean, for example, when he characterizes metaphor as "the omnipresent principle of language"? Are we to understand that all word meanings are figurative? Surely, this seems somewhat exaggerated. That all new words and meanings are figurative? Even this would be difficult to substantiate. Specialized meanings arise from marginal rather than metaphorical extensions, and this appears to be true of semantic generalization as well. There is little of the metaphor in such word-forming processes as clipping, blending, or the addition of derivative suffixes. In this entire area we need clarity of definition, sobriety of attitude, and rigor of method. It is possible that some of the more recent work on meaning, notably that by Ullman, Weinreich, and Fodor and Katz,[8] may have some implications for and applications to these matters. Indeed, it is to be hoped that this will be the case.

Thus far the discussion has been confined chiefly to matters where the principal contribution of the linguist would appear to be in furnishing the literary critic with a series of safeguards against the acceptance of unfounded and untested assumptions, vague and unsupportable definitions, and neglect of easily ascertainable historical fact. This is all-important, but it is also, in a sense at least, somewhat negative. Nevertheless, to the extent that the student of literature interests himself in the language of the literary work, there would seem to be little point in his ignoring the results of present-day systematic study of language, the methods which characterize it, and the hypotheses upon which it is based.

The next question is, how far can we go beyond this, and what, up to the present, has been the outcome of any attempts to do so? From about 1952 on there were a series of summer seminars devoted to studying the application of linguistics to the study of literature, usually held in connection with the Linguistic Institute. Such seminars have been held at the Universities of Michigan, Chicago, Indiana, and Texas. The most exciting event was a Conference on Style, held at Indiana University in April, 1958; the participants included linguists, literary historians and critics, psychologists, and cultural anthropologists. The proceedings of the conference have been published under the title *Language and Style*.[9] The most persistent contributors of publications in the field have been A. A. Hill, Roman Jakobson, Seymour Chatman, and Samuel Levin.

It remains, therefore, to indicate something of the nature of the thinking that has gone on in these papers and articles, to point out areas where the linguist might conceivably have something to contribute, and to suggest what the nature of that contribution might be. Obviously, what the linguist has to contribute is conditioned by the present state of his discipline, in terms of underlying assumptions, working methods, and accomplishments to date, and we must first look at each of these.

With respect to the first of the foregoing, it has already been suggested that the linguist assumes any literary work, from a distich to a novel, to be an utterance, a language act, differentiated from nonliterary utterances by a series or set of characteristics of its own. It follows, therefore, according to the linguists, that such a language act can be systematically examined and described, like any other language act.

The linguist recognizes, however, that the literary work, over and above this fundamental similarity, differs from nonliterary utterances either by reflecting a higher degree of selectivity of certain language features, as would be the case with rhyme, alliteration, etc., or by divergences from the usual linguistic norms. In the light of this, the contribution that the linguist is prepared to make is a precise statement, in his own terms, of the nature of the selectivity or of the divergence.

What is principally needed to accomplish these aims is a sound description and presentation of the norms, put into terms that the nonlinguist can understand and use. Admittedly, this has not always been well done. An instance of a highly casual type of procedure is to be found in Leo Spitzer's *Linguistics and Literary History,* where he tells the reader, "In my reading of modern French novels, I had acquired the habit of underlining expressions which struck me as aberrant from modern French."[10] Then, on the basis of these, he imputes to the aberrent expressions a psychology and ultimately a philosophy which he assumes to underlie the literature and in fact the attitudes and entire *Weltanschauung* of the authors in question. Frankly, I would like something more systematic than this, just as I would have preferred a more refined establishment of phonetic norms from Lynch in his study of the tonality of lyric poetry, which is pre-

sumably based upon the frequency of individual sounds. Norms
are also important in the interpretation of literature which makes
use of social or regional dialects. Whether such norms are to be
mathematically determined or based upon something like the
kernel sentences of generative grammar still remains to be decided. Both methods may well be useful.

So much for what might be called an application of the norma-
tive principle. Let us turn now to the way in which the linguist
proceeds in the analysis of language. Will a characterization of
his working method shed some light upon his possible contribution to the analysis of literature? Three features in particular
should be mentioned: 1) In the past, at least, most study has
proceeded according to levels of structural complexity, moving
generally from the simpler toward the more complicated. Generally, though not universally, this has meant working from phonetics to phonemics, then to morphological or inflectional
features, and finally to syntax. In the light of this, it is scarcely
an accident that prosodic analysis has become a lively issue.
2) On each of these levels, the linguist has attempted to isolate
structurally significant, that is to say meaningful, units through
minimal pairing, the recognition of formal markers, and the
recurrence of identical units. This is essentially a process of seg-
mentation. 3) Finally the linguist seeks to determine the degree
of relationship—whether intimate or remote—among units,
based upon the number of units or kind of units which can follow
any element, and also in terms of the evidence furnished by
analysis undertaken on lower levels. This is usually known as
immediate constituent analysis. Our question then becomes, what
can the linguist do for the analysis of literature in terms of his
method of dealing with language segments and language patterns?

In this connection it is pertinent to indicate how far the science
has progressed in each of these approaches. In recent times ar-

ticulatory phonetics has undergone relatively little change; there have been few new developments. The sound spectrograph has, however, advanced our knowledge of acoustic phonetics considerably, and this may have some possibilities for the study of prosody, metrics, and prose rhythm. The next level above this, represented by phonemics, has had the advantage of some years of speculation and research. Despite certain conflicts in theory and procedure, some of which have arisen just recently, it is on a fairly high level of development. As we proceed to morphology and syntax, our total accomplishment is less well defined and more subject to controversy. This must be kept in mind in any consideration of the potential contributions of linguistics to the study of literature.

One obvious application of phonological studies to the analysis of literature has already been suggested, namely, in the field of prosody and metrics. The basic problem here is that the conventional prosody with which most of us are familiar and try to teach in our elementary literature courses recognizes only two degrees of stress. Many linguists are fairly certain that English has four contrastive stresses. Thus, there seems to be an initial fundamental disagreement on this point. In addition, a good many linguists are inclined to distinguish English from such languages as Spanish and Italian. They characterize the latter as syllable-timed, meaning that in general syllables constitute equivalent or nearly equivalent time units. They consider the English verse foot as fundamentally isochronic in nature, consisting of equal time intervals between primary stresses, with unstressed syllables jammed in between, regardless of number.

These matters have come in for considerable discussion, beginning with the 1956 summer issue of the *Kenyon Review,* which contained articles by Harold Whitehall, Seymour Chatham, Karl Shapiro, and John Crowe Ransome. Since then, Northrop

Frye, W. K. Wimsatt, and Monroe Beardsley have joined the fray, and some others as well.[11] Despite a good many statements and perhaps even more assumptions to the contrary, it is probably fair to say that the linguists have tried to suggest ways of supplementing rather than replacing the traditional modes of metrical analysis, through a recognition of the isochronic principle alongside of the familiar syllabic scrutiny, taking into account the possibility of a greater number of levels of stress, and giving attention to such suprasegmental features of the language as intonation and juncture as well as stress. At the very least it must be conceded that they have injected some new life into an old problem.

On the next level of analysis, the morphological, we must recognize that in the past a number of stylistic studies have sought to arrive at conclusions about the work of certain individual authors or even of an entire period by classifying parts of speech and analyzing vocabulary frequency. The work of Josephine Miles and George U. Yule, to mention only two, fall into this category.[12] Here the difficulty arises in the development of valid sorting techniques and in refining the units to be counted.

As an illustration of some of the difficulties encountered in work of this nature, two comments from an article by Rudolph Von Abele on the poetry of E. E. Cummings may be cited. He writes, "Any analysis is largely the refining of crude concepts, established as it were by 'feel'."[13] If the linguist has any contribution at all to make toward the analysis of literature, it would seem to be in the direction of establishing concepts on the basis of something more tangible than this. It is dubious whether any concept intuitively based at the outset can be satisfactorily refined, no matter what is done to it. To quote Von Abele again, "It is not always easy to decide what is a compound and what is an instance of word mixing."[14] As a matter of fact, it is fairly easy to make this type of decision on the basis of actual reading performances of the poems, since the prosodic features of compounds in English are quite clearly defined and clearly recognizable. Certainly, Louis C. Rus, in his analysis of structural ambiguities in the works of the same poet, was able to employ linguistically valid formal characteristics for this purpose. Moreover, Henry Kahane of the University of Illinois has made use of the techniques of content analysis in studying the style of *The Cid*. This may turn out to be a helpful supplement to the more conventional frequency studies and part-of-speech classifications.

On the broadest and most comprehensive level of analysis we encounter a type of linguistic study which has been termed discourse analysis, the chief attempt thus far on the part of the linguists to deal with segments of language more extensive than the sentence. In it meaning is characterized as "the most probable substitute controlled by the most frequent sequences"—a definition which leaves much to be desired. Here we must also recognize the work of Eugene Dorfman, who has studied French and Spanish epics in terms of the narreme as the functional unit of narrative incident. With respect to the study of these larger structures, the best that can be said is that we are still at an embryonic stage.

At this point, however, we have moved to a point somewhat beyond the needs of the classroom teacher, who must deal with certain stylistic matters in a practical way. On the one hand he needs a tool to characterize the writing, literary or nonliterary, with which the student comes into contact. He wants a method of comparing the prose of Hemingway with that of Faulkner, of characterizing the writing of Dos Passos, of Thomas Wolfe, to say nothing of Arnold, Carlisle, and Pater.

On the productive side, one of his most challenging tasks is to communicate to the student, especially at the upper secondary level and in the beginning college years, some sense of the potential in language. As Francis Christensen has said:

> The chapters on the sentence (in the usual handbook or grammar) all appear to assume that we think naturally in primer sentences, progress naturally to compound sentences, and must be taught to combine the primer sentences into complex sentences —and that complex sentences are the mark of maturity. We need a rhetoric of the sentence that will do more than combine the ideas of primer sentences. We need one that will generate ideas.[15]

Although at this point we seem to be edging over into the province of rhetoric, it is worth nothing that in the past a workable rhetoric has always been based upon sound linguistic analysis, and there is no reason to believe that the situation would be different with respect to present-day English. What appears to be needed is a relatively simple and workable analytic device which can be used and comprehended by the classroom teacher, one which will indicate the syntactic structure of sentences, the frequency of occurrence of certain patterns of word order, the amount and kinds of subordination, the placement of modifying elements.

In this connection I should like to propose that serious consideration be given to a wider use of the analytic model employed by Professor Ruth Strickland in her monograph, *The Language of Elementary School Children,* by Professor Walter Loban in his series of studies on the same topic, and by Professor Kellogg Hunt in his analysis of the writing of elementary and secondary school students.[16] Originally devised by a member of Miss Strickland's staff, named Ekhtiar, it was discussed and refined at a conference in which John Carroll, Nelson Francis, Fred Householder, David Reed, and Harold Whitehall all participated.

Fundamentally a slot and filler type of analysis, it operates on two levels. The first of these analyzes basic clause and sentence structure into fixed slots and movables. The second level indicates the types of satellites and subordinations employed in connection with the fixed and movable elements. Although it is far from being a foolproof or perfect scheme, it can be used and understood by teachers who are not themselves professional linguists. The best proof of this is its use in six dissertations done under Dr. Strickland's direction. Now is the time, it would seem, to reassess the experience with it and to suggest possible improvements.

I hasten to say that I do not consider this, or any other of the possible techniques and processes that I have mentioned, the sole or final answer to the study of style or the evaluation of literature. Criticism remains as an activity in its own right. I would go so far as to say, moreover, that the actual results of the analysis conducted by the linguist will not always or necessarily differ markedly from those obtained by the nonlinguist. What the linguist's methods do have to recommend them is the substitution of an ordered and systematic procedure in dealing with language for what is often vague and undisciplined intuition, a method which pays serious attention to its assumptions about language rather than one which tends to ignore them. And here we find a close parallel to the contribution that linguistics has made to the whole problem of language instruction.

Eight

THE ROLE OF LANGUAGE
IN THE CURRICULUM

IN THE FOREGOING SEVEN CHAPTERS I HAVE TRIED TO SUGGEST various ways in which the systematic study of language, which we know as linguistics, might make a contribution toward the more effective teaching of English in the elementary and secondary schools. We dealt with this vast and almost all-inclusive subject of English in terms of its most important components: grammar, usage, composition, spelling, reading, and literature. In each instance the question was posed approximately in these terms, "How may the discipline of linguistics in its current state be applied to this particular division of the subject matter of English?" It is important to note that from such an examination, no single, simple, or uniform answer emerged.

In connection with the teaching of English grammar and in dealing with problems of usage, the potential applications of linguistics did appear to be relatively direct. We must adapt the results of the best scholarship in the field to the classroom situation. This raises a host of questions concerning the preparation of teachers and the development of teaching materials, including audio-visual aids and programmed instruction.

With respect to the teaching of spelling, reading, composition, and literature, it is evident that in every instance linguistics has a contribution to make, but by no means the sole contribution. The principal problem here is to integrate in the most effective manner possible the linguistic contribution with those from other fields and disciplines. In all of this it is most important not to overrate the achievements of linguistics or to promise too much in the way of possible application. Nor indeed should the accomplishment of the promise of linguistics be underrated, but even so, litotes might be preferable to hyperbole. We should especially avoid the notion that there is a "linguistic method" of teaching any of these phases of English. Sober realism and devastating frankness will in the long run prove to be our best approach.

We can scarcely afford, however, to limit our concern to instruction in English and the ways in which it may be rendered more effective by the application of linguistics. We must think of these matters in the light of the educational process as a whole. To what end do we teach, and try to induce our students to learn, language, literature, and composition? For what purpose are we attempting to make our instruction more effective through the introduction and application of linguistic concepts and procedures? Such questions of basic educational aim must be considered here in order to place the preceding chapters in a proper and broader context.

Of course, there have been many discussions of this nature. Some of them have taken place in connection with the one-week workshops in linguistics conducted over the past few years by the National Council of Teachers of English. Such questions have also arisen in connection with the efforts by several state departments of education to revise the language arts curriculum, notably New York and Pennsylvania. They have been a primary concern in the various curriculum workshops supported by Project English of the U.S. Office of Education.

In most considerations of the question, the justification of the place of language study in the curriculum has centered about two points. The first of these is the centrality of language to the human experience. It is frequently pointed out that language, more than anything else, sets the human race apart from other forms of life in the world. Since it is thus one of our richest resources, an understanding of it, of the way it is structured, the way it functions, and even some aspects of its history, is educationally important and justifiable.

There is also a feeling, widely prevalent in some quarters, that it is better for English teachers to deal with the English language as a recognized part of the subject matter of English than for them to exercise what must essentially be amateur efforts in the subject areas of philosophy, psychology, economics, sociology, and cultural anthropology. This attitude has arisen with particular reference to the content of college freshmen anthologies and to the kind of writing that they stimulate.

Underlying this point of view—with which one need not necessarily agree in its entirety—is the recognition of language as one member of a trinity or triad, with literature (and the necessary reading skills) and composition constituting the other two. Although there is a certain convenience about this threefold division, it does falsify the situation in one sense. Language is the medium for both literature and composition; without language neither would be possible. This merely serves to reinforce what was said earlier about the centrality of language, to the school as well as to the human experience.

Possibly as the result of this very concept, we have seen in recent years the introduction—or more accurately the *re*introduction—of some systematic study of the English language in high school and even elementary school curricula. The new Portland (Oregon) curriculum for college-bound students provides for both the history of the English language and a study of American dialects. The Minnesota Curriculum Center, supported by funds from the U.S. Office of Education, is working toward the development of a language-oriented English curriculum from the seventh grade through the twelfth. A similar project at the University of Buffalo is concerned with the development of language teaching materials for the same span of years. The public schools of Westport, Connecticut, have been working toward this end for a number of years. This is by no means an exhaustive list—there are others as well.

Nor are these curricula being developed in a vacuum. Textbooks and other teaching materials are being devised to serve their needs. Neil Postman, Paul Roberts, and W. Nelson Francis have written textbooks which deal with the English language, both descriptively and historically.[1] Despite certain shortcomings, the treatment of American-English dialects by Jean Malmstrom and Clara Ashley has generally been well received.[2]

All of this is excellent and encouraging, but a discussion of the place of language study in the curriculum which limited itself to merely this kind of running narrative would scarcely arise above a surface approach to the problem. The question merits a more extensive and somewhat deeper exploration than is implicit in the particular developments and the reasoning behind them which has been reported thus far. The title of the present chapter suggests the breadth of approach which I believe that the question demands. It is designed to deal with the place of all language study in the curriculum. It does not specify the English language, nor does it carry the label *linguistics*.

I, too, would begin such a discussion with the centrality of language to the human experience, to our existence as human beings. By serving as a vehicle of communication, language makes cooperation among individuals possible, and in so doing, it serves as the very basis of human society. Writing, too, has made its social contribution by rendering us independent of human memory and of human presence, without benefit of electronic or mechanical aid. Speaker and hearer must be in the same place, at the same time; writer and reader need not.

Proceeding from this essentially social view of the function of language, we must consider next the social order of which we are a part, and the function of education within that society. In our society, as in any other, one important purpose of education is to transmit, to preserve, and to improve our social heritage. Ours happens to be a democratic one. Rightly or wrongly, we believe in it, and understandably, we want to preserve it.

If we grant this, if we are to retain an essentially democratic way of life, if we are to safeguard those aspects of it which we define as freedom, as liberty, as a proper concern for the worth and dignity of the individual, it follows that our principal educational responsibility is to prepare the oncoming generations for intelligent participation and responsible leadership in such a social order. Our vast society, constructed as it is, can survive only as a result of human cooperation on a greater scale than has been attempted up to this time. Language, as we have already said, is a prime factor in this cooperative endeavor.

Unfortunately there are certain features and developing trends in our society which work against this cooperative potential. We occupy a huge area; our population is still growing rapidly. The more people there are and the greater the distances to be spanned, the more difficult cooperative endeavor becomes. Moreover, during the present century, many social problems are no longer local in scope, as they once were, but have become matters demanding national attention. The very titles of the two most recently created cabinet posts, namely health, education, and welfare, and urban affairs, offer striking testimony to our emergent national concerns, again calling for consideration by millions of persons spread over a territory of three million square miles.

Although we have succeeded in overcoming time and space by means of jet travel and electronic tubes, we have not yet adequately prepared ourselves to cope with this change. We can talk with Alaska at a moment's notice, but have we something worthwhile to say, and can we communicate it? This is the kind of Thoreauvian question which does not permit an easy answer. Nowhere were the difficulties in communication and in real understanding more strikingly evidenced than at the 1964 national convention of the Republican party, where the resentment toward radio commentators and news columnists from the eastern part of the country was overwhelming. Mass communications in our present society have a tremendous potential for good—or evil.

In view of the growing complexity and the unfortunate development of these divisive trends in our society, it would seem that the first charge upon our educational system is to develop, in the students who are to be its products, an improved ability to communicate and a will to do so, thus assuring the social cooperation necessary for our continued future existence. There is a productive and a receptive aspect of the communicative processes. The first demands an articulate public. The second calls for a critical public. Needless to say, we have not yet achieved either of them for more than a minority of those whom we have tried to educate. A minority is insufficient to meet our needs.

I have spoken in a previous chapter of our general inarticulateness. Too many of us shrink from the lectern and put down a pen with dismay when a situation demands precise and well reasoned expression. Too often in public and in private life we feel no responsibility to the language in which we try to communicate. In the Baconian terminology, we have become neither ready nor exact men.

Again, at the risk of repetition, I must point out that as a nation we are too indifferent and too unsophisticated with respect to what we hear and read. We are not a nation of critical readers, nor are we immune to the verbal tricks and skills of the huckster, be he commercially or politically inspired. We are tolerant of nonsense, a notoriously easy prey to slogans, in both our political and our economic life. We forgive lapses in logic quite as easily as we forgive lapses in taste, if indeed we recognize either of them as lapses. A truly critical audience at a national meeting, representing every section of the country, would have hooted off the stage the author of such a pretentious oratorical flight as "hawkers of hate, purveyors of prejudice, fabricators of fear." Indeed the speaker was jeered, but not because of his rhetorical bombast.

The development of our nation and of our social order is at a point where we can no longer afford the ease and laziness of the inarticulate, the lack of a critical sense, the preservation of a wide-eyed naivete. We shall have to amend these faults or run the risk of forfeiting our democratic heritage, of falling into the toils of a dictatorship or of thought control of some kind, whatever form it may take.

Improving the language command of the almost fifty million enrolled in our schools is no small task. It is, in fact, a major one, which will involve a judicious combination of linguistics, rhetoric, and logic.

Training in the basic language patterns and adequate exercise in ways of expanding and manipulating them is the primary element in developing an articulate public. We must find out how to do this for speakers of substandard as well as standard English, for those who are at a cultural disadvantage as well as those who are culturally favored. The two approaches may have to be quite different, and we must make use of all the resources of linguistics to help us devise the most effective teaching procedures. Unless we do, the leadership we shall need over the next two or three decades will not emerge.

On the receptive side of language, we shall have to give increased attention to logic, to guard us from the intentional and unintentional flaws of those who seek to move us to action. We must depend heavily upon semantics to provide us with armor to protect ourselves from and weapons to defeat the verbal juggler. To put it somewhat brutally, we must frighten our men of affairs into logic, into intellectual and verbal integrity.

At the same time we must be careful not to develop one or more generations of rigid authoritarians or linguistic snobs, since this leads to fear and paralysis in the use of language. This can be avoided, however, by inculcating in our students an informed and a tolerant view about standards of usage, about prestige dialects and their development, about the place of social and regional dialects in our society and how they function as a reflection of it. In fact, we must learn to take full advantage both of psycholinguistics and sociolinguistics as well as linguistics proper.

In a sense the greatest and most important task falls to the rhetorician. Properly considered, rhetoric must be presented as something more than a collection of verbal devices calculated to make language appealing and persuasive. It has a moral charge as well. It should develop in the student both a sense of responsibility toward the language he uses and toward the soundness and justice of the ideas he intends to communicate.

Thus far the place of language in the curriculum has been considered from a strictly national and monolingual point of view. But no man is an island, nor is a nation any longer. It is not only our national life which daily becomes more complex, more tension-ridden, more beset with difficult problems. This applies equally to the world situation and to our relationships with the rest of the world, as a glance at any daily newspaper will demonstrate all too clearly. Here the language barrier adds a further complicating factor. The difficulties of communication within a single language are compounded many times over when we must arrive at a common understanding through the use of two or more languages.

The settlement of our recent dispute with Panama was delayed for weeks because of a misinterpretation of the deceptive English-Spanish cognates *discuss* and *discutar, negotiate* and *negociar.* All too often we have been led into difficulties because we failed to realize that French *demander* is less peremptory than the English *demand.* But difficulties arise not only from mistranslation but also from the varying degrees of prestige accorded to various languages within a multilingual nation. What the national language is to be has become a political issue both in India and in Ceylon. At one time or another, Belgium has been bitterly divided over the language question. And even if the choice of the national language is not a matter of debate, the presence of two or more languages within a country can be a divisive force, the splendid record of the Swiss notwithstanding.

We may as well recognize that a single world language is not likely to be accepted or established in the foreseeable future. The experiments over the past seventy-five years with such artificial languages as Esperanto, Ido, Volapuk, and others have not been encouraging in their results. The current international situation appears to favor an extensive future development for at least three or four existing languages rather than one, as auxiliary or second languages. But we shall have to learn many others if we really want to understand and make ourselves understood over the vast area of the globe. It is possible to order a meal in Warsaw or Bucharest in a judicious combination of English, French, and German; it is not possible to talk with the man in the street and get some notion of what he thinks and feels. And, of course, this is even more true of Bangkok and Kampala. It has been said by an acute observer of language problems that by the year 2000, a person who does not want to be relegated to a menial or at best a humdrum place in our society will have to be able to use three or four languages. Unfortunately, he will scarcely be in a position to predict, during his school years, which languages his position in life will call upon him to use. Moreover, languages not now regularly taught in our schools are assuming more and more importance, and in all likelihood will continue to do so.

What, then, are the schools to do in order to meet this kind of situation? Suppose a student spends some years acquiring Arabic and he finds that what he really needs is Chinese or Finnish. What we shall have to do to avoid this potentially cruel jest is to concentrate not so much upon the mastery of one foreign language or two as to impart an understanding of *language* and of the way in which other languages can be learned. It is an approach, a language-learning technique that we shall have to get across to our students.

The range of what we today consider to be world languages encompasses such widely diverse languages from the point of view of structure as Chinese, Hindi, Russian, and Arabic, as well as the more familiar French, German, Italian, Spanish, and Portuguese. But Chinese is a tone language. Both Hindi and Russian are highly inflected, by our standards. Arabic has a sound system far different from our own.

How do we go about preparing large numbers of students to acquire one or another of these languages when the occasion demands? The starting point is, as has already been suggested, an understanding of language, of its structure and operation. The recognition that every language has its system, that the system can be described in understandable terms, combined with the realization that somehow every child is capable of learning his mother tongue and does learn it, will go far toward overcoming the glottophobia (or xenophobia) so firmly embedded in our national consciousness. Convincing the mass of our students of this will take us much closer to linguistics than anything we have introduced in the schools so far. But we can only begin in terms of the language the pupil knows and uses—English. Much of it will have to be communicated at an early stage of the educational process, probably in the elementary school. We shall simply have to develop ways of communicating these matters. If mathematical set theory can be presented to the preadolescent, so can any number of linguistic concepts.

As we look forward to our life in the coming decades, a third area emerges in which language is destined to play a major role. Even now we have accepted the fact that people generally will have more time on their hands, as a consequence of increasing mechanization and automation. Talk about a thirty-five-hour working week is now so common that it no longer surprises us when we hear it. It is only when the figure goes down to thirty or twenty-five that we begin to register shock and wonder what people will do to fill up the remaining eighty-seven waking hours in a seven-day span. Our traditional statements of educational objectives have always included as an important goal the pious phrase, "worthy use of leisure time," but we really have done little about it. Now we shall have to begin to take it seriously. Certainly as a society we cannot run the risk of filling up the increased time at our disposal with the vapid, the thrill for the sake of thrill, the purely physical excitation. Basket weaving, B-grade movies, and beer can scarcely be expected to occupy the hours with satisfaction to many. If history teaches us anything, a failure here would seem to be an invitation to the decay of our civilization and culture.

The time would seem to be ripe, therefore, for a rediscovery of literature, among other things of course, in all the forms that it has traditionally assumed. Nor need we limit ourselves to the traditional. Let us transfer the standards of excellence we demand and are accustomed to in the drama and the novel to the newer forms of expression, the livelier arts, the mass media, or whatever one may wish to call them. If we develop a mature criticism, a public taste, and a vocal public in connection with these media, standards of excellence will emerge. We shall get better vehicles, grudgingly of course, but we shall get them. This will require a greater sensitivity to language than we have succeeded in developing today in most of our students, and sadly enough, in many of our teachers.

Success here, and it is socially not only desirable but necessary, will depend upon what has previously been called the development of an instinctive regard for style in language, something we have failed to acquire as a people. A few men in public life in our time have had it, but for the most part we accept the clumsy, the ponderous, the pretentious without knowing that it is so. Much of the country lacks a critical ear and a cultivated voice, and indeed it feels—mistakenly, of course—that it is somehow democratic to be this way. There are historical reasons for this feeling and perhaps even for the shortcoming, but they do not constitute an argument for continuation. To improve the situation will require more, and a different kind of attention to language than we have given in the past. We shall need a linguistic, a rhetoric, and a stylistic—all adapted to our time and needs.

Obviously this is an ambitious program. It will require time and effort, a great amount of both. In all justice to those interested in other parts of the curriculum, we must ask ourselves where the time is to be found. At the expense of what? How do we make room for this increased attention to language?

Part of the answer must lie in a greater effectiveness of and efficiency in presentation than we now achieve. Our teaching and repeated reteaching of the elements of an ill-fitting grammar has little to commend it. Time can be saved here. There is reason to believe that for many pupils the teaching of reading and of spelling can be accelerated. The program in literature might be reexamined to good effect.

We may also have to discard some elements which now have a place in our teaching program. It is obvious that we cannot achieve the universal in one school year, or for that matter in the curriculum as a whole. We shall have to begin to make choices, to establish priorities and sequences, to eliminate the nonessential.

In this connection it is well for us to recall the former place of language study in education. The grammar school was originally so called because grammar was the most important subject in it. Virtually half of the medieval university curriculum, in fact the entire program for the baccalaureate, dealt with language in one way or another: the trivium consisted of grammar, rhetoric, and logic. Thus, what has really been the chief topic of discussion in this chapter, the centrality of language to the human experience, was clearly reflected by the educational practice of the Middle Ages. It may well be that language will of necessity resume in our culture the primacy which it had prior to the Renaissance, when materialism and emphasis upon the physical world diverted attention from it.

Finally, we must not be led into the error of assessing the total learning potential, the knowledge or behavior of a people, solely in terms of what is taught in the classroom. For example, American men are, with a few notable exceptions, what might be called mechanically literate. They have a feel for engines and machinery. They seem to know what makes wheels turn, what makes parts fit together, and what to do if the wheels won't turn or the parts don't fit. One can almost see this particular aptness progress, generation by generation. It is not taught, directly or indirectly. The boys simply absorb it. It appears to be an instance of education by osmosis.

American women also seem to have, though in a lesser degree, something of an instinct for color combination, a flair for the decorative, a way of making things genuinely attractive—when they are not deluded or hoodwinked by professional fashion designers and interior decorators. People in certain other countries have an instinctive sense with respect to painting and music. Scratch an Englishman and you find an amateur archaeologist, and a pretty good one at that.

I cannot believe that these are inherited, racial, or national traits. They seem to stem rather from an environment so pervasive that it plays upon the individual from childhood on. There is no reason why a sensitivity to language, an articulateness, a linguistic competence should not also in time become so much an integral part of the atmosphere that it would not operate in a like manner.

I have chosen to deal with the role of language in the curriculum in these broad terms, with more attention to theory than to details of application, because I am convinced that the demands of the future upon the language competence of literally millions of our countrymen will be so stringent, so critical, so necessary to our continued functioning as a democracy and as a potent force in a world in crisis that we shall have to gear our education to them. We shall, as I have said, be faced with the necessity of making many decisions: what to teach, when, where, and how to teach it. But only in the light of a broad, an informed, a forward-looking view of the place of language in our culture and in human society can these decisions be made with adequate foresight and intelligence.

We shall need, of course, to think precisely, even to think small, but it must always be in the context of a large view of the future of this country and of mankind. And in all of this, teachers of English and linguists have a challenging role to play, and an urgent responsibility to play it not merely well but superbly.

Notes

Index

Notes

2. CURRENT APPROACHES TO ENGLISH GRAMMAR

1. Allen H. Weld, *English Grammar*, 25th ed., (Auburn, N.Y., 1848), Preface, p. iii.

2. Secondary School Examinations Council, *The Examining of English Language* (London, 1964), p. 2.

3. Goold Brown, *The Grammar of English Grammars*, 9th ed. (New York, 1865), p. 22.

4. Ibid., p. 112.

5. Ibid., p. 25.

6. Ibid., p. 112.

7. *Examining of English Language*, p. 3.

8. Henry Sweet, *A New English Grammar* (Oxford, 1891), Preface, p. xii.

9. Harold E. Palmer, *A Grammar of Spoken English* (Cambridge, 1924).

10. Otto Jespersen, *A Modern English Grammar* (Heidelberg, 1927), II, 6.

11. Janet R. Aiken, *A New Plan of English Grammar* (New York, 1933).

12. Sweet, *New English Grammar*, p. 5.

13. Quoted from the mimeographed text of a lecture given to the Chicago College English Association at its annual fall conference on November 14, 1964.

14. Noam Chomsky, *Syntactic Structures* ('S-Gravenhage, 1957).

15. Ibid., pp. 106-107.

16. Emmon Bach, *An Introduction to Transformational Grammars* (New York, 1964), p. 64.

3. USAGE: VARIETIES, LEVELS, AND STYLES

1. George Philip Krapp, *Modern English: Its Growth and Present Use* (New York, 1909), pp. 10-14, 149-154, 325-29; Sterling A. Leonard and H. Y. Moffett, "Current Definitions of Levels in English Usage," *English Journal*, 16 (May, 1927), 345-59.

2. John S. Kenyon, "Levels of Speech and Colloquial English," *English Journal*, 37 (January, 1948), 25-31; "Cultural Levels and Functional Varieties of English," *College English*, 10 (October, 1948), 31-36.

3. Kenyon, "Cultural Levels," p. 31.

4. Ibid.

5. Ibid.

6. Ibid.

7. Such definitions for these terms as may be found in school textbooks often make the point that they consist of words which are not recognized parts of the language and are therefore not found in dictionaries, or constructions which do not conform even to the rules of informal grammar, and that slang predominates. These ascriptions —they can scarcely be called definitions—are incorrect on virtually all counts. Authoritative dictionaries do include substandard locutions. It is jargon and argot rather than slang which is heavily present, and they fail to recognize that every social and regional dialect has a grammar to which the speakers of that dialect conform, though it may not be the grammar of the prestige dialect.

8. Kenyon, "Cultural Levels," p. 31.

9. Ibid.

10. Martin Joos, *The Five Clocks* (Bloomington, Ind., 1962), Indiana University Research Center in Anthropology, Folklore, and Linguistics, Publication 22.

11. *Webster's Third New International Dictionary* (Springfield, Mass., 1961), Preface, p. 6a/2.

12. Ibid.

13. Ibid., p. 19a, Sec. 8.2.2.
14. Ibid., p. 19a, Sec. 8.2.3.

4. USAGE: FINDING AND INTERPRETING THE FACTS

1. Wilson Follett, "Sabotage in Springfield," *The Atlantic*, 209 (January, 1962), 73-77.

2. Sheridan Baker, "The Error of Ain't," *College English*, 26 (November, 1964), 91-104.

3. E. Bagby Atwood, *A Survey of Verb Forms in the Eastern United States* (Ann Arbor, Mich., 1953), pp. 30-31.

4. Sir William Craigie and James R. Hulbert, eds., *A Dictionary of American English on Historical Principles*, 4 vols. (Chicago, 1938-1944).

5. Mitford M. Mathews, ed., *A Dictionary of Americanisms*, 2 vols. (Chicago, 1951).

6. Hans Kurath, ed., *Linguistic Atlas of New England*, 3 vols. in 6 (Providence, R.I., 1939-43).

7. Hans Kurath, *A Word Geography of the Eastern United States* (Ann Arbor, Mich., 1949).

8. Hans Kurath and Raven I. McDavid, Jr., *The Pronunciation of English in the Atlantic States* (Ann Arbor, Mich., 1961).

9. Margaret M. Bryant, *Current American Usage* (New York, 1962).

10. Bergen and Cornelia Evans, *A Dictionary of Contemporary American Usage* (New York, 1957).

11. Henry W. Fowler, *A Dictionary of Modern English Usage* (Oxford, 1926). A second edition, revised and modernized by Sir Ernest Gowers, appeared in 1965. To quote the reviser, "The illustrative quotations have been pruned in several articles, and passages where the same subject is dealt with in more than one article have been omitted." Preface to the revised edition, p. ix.

12. Herbert W. Horwill, *A Dictionary of Modern American Usage* (Oxford, 1935).

13. Margaret Nicholson, *A Dictionary of American-English Usage* (New York, 1957).

14. Fowler, *Modern English Usage*, p. 182. Sir Ernest Gowers, in the revised edition, alters the last sentence to read, "That is unfortunate, for when the primary and the popular meanings are at odds, the latter tends to corrupt the former."

15. Evans, *Dictionary of Contemporary American Usage*, Preface, p. vi.

16. Ibid., p. v.

17. Ibid., p. vii.

18. Ibid., pp. 276-77.

19. Sterling A. Leonard, *Current English Usage*, English Monograph No. 1, National Council of Teachers of English (Chicago, 1932). A. H. Marckwardt and Fred Walcott in *Facts About Current English Usage*, English Monograph No. 7, National Council of Teachers of English (New York, 1938), gave the available factual evidence of usage status on the same items which were included in the Leonard monograph.

20. Leonard, *Current English Usage*, p. 161.

21. Otto Jespersen, *A Modern English Grammar on Historical Principles,* 8 vols. (Copenhagen, 1909-1949), II, 170-72.

22. George O. Curme, *Syntax* (New York, 1931), pp. 310-12.

23. Charles C. Fries, *American English Grammar*, English Monograph No. 10, National Council of Teachers of English (New York, 1940).

24. Ibid., p. 84.

5. Linguistic and the Teaching of Composition

1. Charles F. Hockett, *Introduction to Modern Linguistics* (New York, 1958), p. 360.

2. The most recent discussions on this point will be found in Ruth G. Strickland, *The Language of Elementary School Children*, Bulletin of the School of Education, Indiana University, Vol. 38, No. 4 (July, 1962), pp. 44-61. See also Kellogg W. Hunt, *Differences in Grammatical Structures Written at Three Grade Levels*, National Council of Teachers of English, 1965.

3. Ruth H. Weir, *Language in the Crib* (The Hague, 1962).

4. Charles C. Fries, *The Structure of English* (New York, 1952), pp. 144-72.

5. Norman C. Stageberg, "Some Structural Ambiguities," *English Journal*, 47 (November, 1958), 479-86.

6. Donald J. Lloyd and Harry R. Warfel, *American English in Its Cultural Setting* (New York, 1956).

7. *Understanding Grammar* (New York, 1954); *Patterns of English* (New York, 1956); *Understanding English* (New York, 1958); *English Sentences* (New York, 1962); *English Syntax* (New York, 1964).

8. Sister Mary Aquin, "A Structural Approach to the Freshman Theme," *College Composition and Communication* 11 (February, 1960): 43-50.

9. Francis Christensen, "A Generative Rhetoric of the Sentence," *College Composition and Communication* 14 (October, 1963): 155-61; "A Generative Rhetoric of the Paragraph," *College Composition and Communication* 16 (October, 1965): 144-56.

6. LINGUISTICS AND THE TEACHING OF SPELLING AND READING

1. Leonard Bloomfield, "Linguistics and Reading," *Elementary English Review*, 19 (April-May, 1942), 125-34, 183-86.

2. Leonard Bloomfield, "Why a Linguistic Society?" *Language*, 1 (1925), 4-5.

3. George L. Trager and Henry Lee Smith, Jr., *An Outline of English Structure* (Norman, Okla., 1951), pp. 14-27.

4. Henry W. Fowler, *A Dictionary of Modern English Usage* (Oxford, 1926), p. 415. The quotation is reprinted without change in the recently revised edition by Sir Ernest Gowers.

5. Ruth G. Strickland, *The Language of Elementary School Children*, Bulletin of the School of Education, Indiana University, Vol. 38, No. 4 (July, 1962).

6. Walter D. Loban, *The Language of Elementary School Children*, National Council of Teachers of English, Research Report No. 1, 1963. This is the first of a series of longitudinal studies which Professor Loban has carried on with the same group of children, covering

their entire elementary and secondary school careers. The subsequent volumes are in preparation.

7. Carl A. Lefevre, "A Longer Look at *Let's Read,*" *Elementary English*, 41 (March, 1964), 203.

7. LINGUISTICS AND THE STUDY OF LITERATURE

1. Philip Wheelwright, "Poetry, Myth, and Reality," in *The Language of Poetry*, ed. by Allen Tate (Princeton, 1942), pp. 13-15.

2. John Crowe Ransom, *The World's Body* (New York, 1938), p. 241.

3. Ibid., p. 283.

4. Carl R. Woodring, "Onomatopoeia and Other Sounds in Poetry," *College English*, 14 (January, 1953), 210. See also James Lynch, "The Tonality of Lyric Poetry," *Word*, 9 (December, 1953), 225-240.

5. Woodring, "Onomatopoeia," p. 209.

6. Cleanth Brooks, *The Well Wrought Urn* (New York, 1947), p. 8.

7. Frederick W. Bateson, *English Poetry and the English Language* (Oxford, 1934).

8. Jerrold J. Katz and Jerry A. Fodor, "The Structure of a Semantic Theory," *Language*, 39 (April-June, 1963), 170-210. Stephen Ullman, "Descriptive Semantics and Linguistic Typology," *Word*, 9 (December, 1953), 225-241. Uriel Weinreich, "On the Semantic Structure of Language," in *Universals of Language*, ed. J. H. Greenberg (Cambridge, Mass., 1963).

9. Thomas A. Sebeok, ed., *Style in Language* (Cambridge, Mass., 1960).

10. Leo Spitzer, *Linguistics and Literary History* (Princeton, 1948), pp. 11-13.

11. W. K. Wimsatt and Monroe Beardsley, "The Concept of Meter: An Exercise in Abstraction," *PMLA*, 74 (June, 1959), 590-91. Monroe Beardsley, *Aesthetics* (New York, 1958), pp. 90-110. Northrop Frye, *Anatomy of Criticism* (Princeton, 1957), pp. 250-60.

12. Josephine Miles, *The Primary Language of Poetry* (Berkeley,

1948); *Renaissance, Eighteenth-Century and Modern Language in English Poetry* (Berkeley, 1960). George U. Yule, *The Statistical Study of Literary Vocabulary* (Cambridge, England, 1944).

13. Rudolph Von Abele, " 'Only to Grow': Change in the Poetry of E. E. Cummings," *PMLA*, 70 (December, 1955), 914.

14. Ibid., p. 920.

15. Francis Christensen, "A Generative Rhetoric of the Sentence," *College Composition and Communication*, 14 (October, 1963), 155.

16. Ruth G. Strickland, *The Language of Elementary School Children* (Bloomington, 1962). Walter D. Loban, *The Language of Elementary School Children*, National Council of Teachers of English, 1963. Kellogg W. Hunt, *Differences in Grammatical Structure at Three Grade Levels*, National Council of Teachers of English, 1965.

8. The Role of Language in the Curriculum

1. Jean Malmstrom and Annabel Ashley, *Dialects USA*, National Council of Teachers of English, 1963.

2. W. Nelson Francis, *The English Language* (New York, 1965). Neil Postman is the editor, consultant, and part author of a series of five textbooks published from 1963 to 1966 by Holt, Rinehart and Winston. The titles are *Discovering Your Language, Exploring Your Language, The Uses of Language, The Language of Discovery, Language and Systems*. Books by Paul Roberts are listed in footnote 7, Chapter V.

Index

Analysis. *See* Linguistic analysis

Colloquial English. *See* Usage
Composition: Conference on College, and Communication, 10; motivation of students, 68-69; theme writing, 68-69; problems in teaching of, and possible solutions, 68-70, 75-76, 81-84; emphasis on expository and argumentative writing, 69, 70, 76; principle aims of, 71-75; language patterns in, 75-83; intonation, stress, and juncture, 77, 83; studies related to, 77-84 *passim*
Connotation, 109-113
Communication: Conference on College Composition and, 10; need to improve, 126-27; difficulties of, compounded, 130
Criticism, literary, 100-121 *passim* —"new," 101-104
Critics and linguists views: on linguistic primitivism, 102-104; on primacy of spoken language, 103; on poets as makers or remakers of language, 104-108; on relationship of sound to meaning, 107-108; on denotation and connotation, 109-113; on metaphor, 109, 112-13; on figurative use of language, 112-13
Curriculum: of medieval universities, 7-8, 134; decline of grammar in, 7-8; language in, 27, 70, 129, 134; language-oriented, 124-25; experimental changes in, 124-25; changes needed in, 131-34 *passim*

Denotation, 109-113
Diction, 70, 83
Dictionaries: guides to usage, 33-34, 45, 83-84, 105; use of, in teaching English, 50-60; historical, 105
Dialect, 104, 106
Dialects: social, 35, 129; regional, 35, 57, 129; class, 35-36, 47; non-linguistic factors in, 36; prestige, 36, 129; local, 38; non-standard, 80; study of, 125

Education: basic aims, purposes, and objectives, 123, 126, 132; articulateness, essential ingredient in, 67

Foreign-language study, revamped, 4
—teachers, problems and goals in common with English teachers, 4-5

147

—words, influx into English, 89
Foreign languages, misinterpretation of cognates, 130
Formal English. *See* Usage
Fowler, H. W., 58-60, 93-94

Grammar: folklore about, 7; declining role of, in curriculum, 7-8, 28; in medieval university curriculum, 7-8, 134; changing focus of, 7-8; tool for study of English, 7-8; functional vs. formal, 8; discussion of, by professional journals and organizations, 11; approaches to, 11-12; as corrective device, 14; *mentioned* 10, 122
—generative: defined, 23-24; limitations of transformations, 24-25; rhetoric of the paragraph, 69; approach to rhetoric, 82; structural linguistics of, 83
—philological-historical: differences from traditional, 18; phonology as basis of, 18; importance of usage in, 19-20
—structuralist: defined, 20-21; patterned vocal behavior, 21; analysis of English phonology, 21-22; descriptive analytic, 22; descriptive synthetic, 22; weakness in handling syntax, 23
—traditional; emphasis on writing, 12-13; defined, 13; negative procedure in, 14; language analysis in, 14; syntax in, 14; parsing in, 14, 17; parts of speech in, 16; rejection of usage, 16; objections to, 16-18
—transformational: defined, 23; use of transformations, 24; syntax in, 25
Grammarians: traditional, 14-15; philological-historical, 18-20; structuralists, 20-23; generative, 23-25. *See also* Language scholars
Grammars, 64-65

Grammatical classification and description, 16, 17, 19

Informal English. *See* Usage
Initial Teaching Alphabet, 92

Jargon, 42-43, 44
Joos, Martin, 40-45

Kenyon, John S., 35, 36-40, 44, 46
Knowledge explosion, 3-4

Language: recent developments in systematic study of, 4; skills, 5; aim of teaching, 5; attitudes toward, 5, 74-75, 77, 81, 84, 90, 102, 121; assumptions about, 5, 121; beginnings of language study, 13; emphasis on written, 13-14; analysis in traditional grammar, 14; defined by structuralists, 21; viewed as vocal behavior, 21; in curriculum, 27, 70, 129, 134, 135; historical study of, 36; need for sensitivity to, 47, 48, 71-72, 135; public taste in, 72-73, 133; structure of, 83, 102, 105, 116, 120; as a literary medium, 100; use of, by authors, 102; primitive, 103; poets' creating or remaking of, 104-106; lack of influence on by individuals, 105-107; figurative use of, 109-113; linguistic analysis of, 116; centrality of, to human experience, 124, 125, 134; critical and articulate public needed for, 127-28; future importance of, 130-33; 135; national disputes over, 131; understanding of, 131
Language-learning: need for techniques for, 131; unrelated to paradigmatic or deductive learning, 78
Language-pattern expansion, 81-83
Language patterns: in composition,

Language patterns—*Cont.*
75-83; syntactical, 97, 120; phonemic-graphemic, 96; structural,
97; intonation, 98; training in
basic, 128
Language scholars: H. W. Fowler,
58-60, 93-94; Martin Joos, 40-45;
John S. Kenyon, 35, 36-40, 44,
46; *others mentioned passim*
Languages, artificial, 131
Linguistic analysis: of English phonology, 21; methods of, of language, 116-21; immediate constituent type of, 116; content
type of, 116; discourse type of,
119; slot and filler type of, 121.
See also Literature, linguistic
analysis of
—anxiety, 73-74
—atlases, 54, 56, 57
—development of a child, 77-80
—geography, 35
—innovation, 28-30
—"method" or "methods," fallacy
of, 66, 70, 123
—norms, need for, 115, 116
—primitivism, 102
—structure, 83, 102. *See also* Language patterns
—studies, 77-98 *passim,* 113, 118-
21 *passim*
Linguistics: discussion of, by professional journals and organizations, 10, 11, 36, 60-63 *passim,*
81, 85, 114, 123; separation of,
from teaching of literature, 101;
historical, 35; structural, 108;
state of the discipline, 114-16
Linguists. *See* Critics and linguists;
Language scholars
Literature: separation from teaching of linguistics, 101; differs
from nonliterary writing, 101,
115; linguistic studies related to,
118-21; mentioned, 66, 124, 134
—linguistic analysis of: prosody,

117; prose rhythm, 117; morphology, 117; verse foot, 117;
metrics, 117-18; degrees of stress,
117, 118; isochronic principle,
117, 118; stylistic studies, 118;
vocabulary frequency, 118; levels
of, 118
—Literary criticism. *See* Criticism,
literary
Logic: in medieval university curriculum, 7-8, 134; lapses in, 128;
need for, 129

Meaning: linguistic studies related
to, 113; fallacies in correlation
with sound, 107; differences in
vocabularies of science and poetry, 109; diacronic changes in,
111
Metaphor, 109-113
Modern Language Association, 63

National Council of Teachers of
English, 10, 61, 63, 123

Orm, an English monk, 82
orthography, 90

Parsing, 14-15, 17
Philological study, 100
Phonemic-graphemic: relationships,
95; correspondence patterns of,
96
Phonemics, 117
Phonetic norms, need for, 115, 116
Phonetics: teachers' need for, 78;
articulatory, 116-17; accoustic,
117
Phonological analysis, 21, 87-94
—studies, 117
—system, child's mastery of, 78, 95
Phonology, in philological-historical grammar, 18; in structuralist
grammar, 21; analysis of, 21
Poets: remaking of language, 104-
105

Poetry, vocabulary of, 109; analysis of E. E. Cummings, 118

Prague School of Linguistics, 20

Population explosion, impact of, 3-4

Professional journals, 10, 11, 36, 60, 81, 114

Professional meetings, 10, 11, 104, 123

Professional organizations, 36, 61-63, 85, 123

Project English, 123

Pronunciation shifts, 88-90, 91-92

Public oratory, 71, 72

Public taste, in language, 72-73

Reading, teaching of: lack of "linguistic methods" for, 70; confusion with language learning, 78, 95; linguistic studies related to, 85-98 passim; language historians contributions to, 86; source of difficulties in, 87-94; Initial Teaching Alphabet for, 92; effect of television on, 96; use of minimal contrasts in, 96-97; need for acceleration of, 134

References for English teachers: linguistic atlases, 54, 56, 57; compendiums of usage, 54-56; grammars, 64-65. See also Dictionaries

Rhetoric, generative, 69, 82, 120, 129, 133, 134. See also Grammar, generative

Secondary School Examinations Council (Great Britain), 11, 17

Semantics: problem of meaning, 108; theory of semantic development, 111; semantic generalization, 113; future need for, 129

Slang. See Usage

Sound: fallacies in correlations with meaning, 107; suggestive values of, vary, 108

Spelling, teaching of: fallacy of

"linguistic methods" for, 70; language historian's contribution to, 86; linguistic studies related to, 86-98 passim; use of minimal contrasts in, 96-97

—reforms, 88-89, 92-94

Speech: primacy of, 21, 75, 103; role in the study of grammar, 13; relationship to writer, 75-77, 85; data needed on, 76

Standard English. See Usage

Standards of English, decline in British, 11

Structuralism. See Grammar, structuralist

Structure. See Language, structure of; Language patterns, structural

Style: in writing, 72-73; child development of, 80, 81; Conference on, 114; in the classroom, 121, 133. See also Usage, styles of

Syntax: in traditional grammar, 14; and form, 64-65; weakness of, in structural grammar, 23; in analysis of literature, 116; in transformational grammar, 25. See also Language patterns, syntactical

Usage: rejection of, 16; acceptance of, 19-20; emphasis on, 27; varieties of, 28-30; changing concepts of, 30-47; acceptable vs. unacceptable, dichotomy in, 33; style shift in, 44; current, 49; compendiums of, 54-56; folk speech, 57

—levels of: Modern, 19; Colloquial, 31-34 passim, 38-40, 41, 45; Illiterate, 31, 32, 37-38, 46, 63; Vulgar, 31, 32, 38; Informal, 31-36; Popular, 31, 38; slang, 32, 38, 42, 43; Literary, 31; Formal, 31, 34, 39; historical, 36; cultural, 36-38 passim, 74; functional, 36-39; Standard, 37-38, 46-57, 80, 106,

Usage—levels of—*Cont.*
128; Substandard, 37-38, 46, 80; Semiformal, 76; ungrammatical, 58

—Styles of: casual, 40, 41, 42, 45; consultative, 40-41, 42, 43, 44, 45; intimate, 40, 42; frozen, 40, 43-44, 45; formal, 40, 43-44, 45, 63; jargon, 42-43, 44

Vocabulary, growth and development, 104-113; differences between poetic and scientific, 109-110

Vowels: relationships of sounds and symbols, 87, 93; vowel shift, 88

Webster, Noah, 93

Webster's Third New International Dictionary, debate over, 50-56, 68

Writing: emphasis on, 13-14; considered secondary in structuralist grammar, 21; lack of, 72, 127; fear of, 72-74; relationship to speech, 75-77, 85, 127; data needed on, 76; devices used in, 77. *See also* Composition